15 Days of Prayer
With Saint Bernard

Also in the *15 Days of Prayer* collection:

15 DAYS OF PRAYER
WITH
Saint Bernard

PIERRE-YVES EMERY, BROTHER OF TAIZÉ

Translated by Victoria Hébert and Denis Sabourin

Liguori
LIGUORI, MISSOURI

Published by Liguori Publications
Liguori, Missouri
http://www.liguori.org

This book is a translation of *Prier 15 Jours Avec Saint Bernard*, published by Nouvelle Cité, 1995, Montrouge, France.

Library of Congress Cataloging-in-Publication Data

Emery, Pierre-Yves.
    [Prier 15 jours avec Saint Bernard. English]
    15 days of prayer with Saint Bernard / Pierre-Yves Emery ; translated by Victoria Hébert and Denis Sabourin. — 1st English ed.
        p.   cm.
    Includes bibliographical references.
    ISBN 0-7648-0574-6
    1. Bernard, of Clairvaux, Saint, 1090 or 91–1153—Meditations. 2. Spiritual life—Catholic Church. I. Title: Fifteen days of prayer with Saint Bernard. II. Title.

BX4700.B5 E44 2000
269'.6—dc21   99-056415

Printed in the United States of America
04 03 02 01 00   5 4 3 2 1
First English Edition 2000

Table of Contents

How to Use This Book

AN OLD CHINESE PROVERB, or at least what I am able to recall of what is supposed to be an old Chinese proverb, goes something like this: "Even a journey of a thousand miles begins with a single step." When you think about it, the truth of the proverb is obvious. It is impossible to begin any project, let alone a journey, without taking the first step. I think it might also be true, although I cannot recall if another Chinese proverb says it, "that the first step is often the hardest." Or, as someone else once observed, "the distance between a thought and the corresponding action needed to implement the idea takes the most energy." I don't know who shared that perception with me but I am certain it was not an old Chinese master!

With this ancient proverbial wisdom, and the not-so-ancient wisdom of an unknown contemporary sage still fresh, we move from proverbs to presumptions. How do these relate to the task before us?

I am presuming that if you are reading this introduction it is because you are contemplating a journey. My presumption is that you are preparing for a spiritual journey and that you have taken at least some of the first steps necessary to prepare for this journey. I also presume, and please excuse me if I am making too many presumptions, that in your preparation for the spiritual journey you have determined that you need a guide.

From deep within the recesses of your deepest self, there was something that called you to consider Saint Bernard as a potential companion. If my presumptions are correct, may I congratulate you on this decision? I think you have made a wise choice, a choice that can be confirmed by yet another source of wisdom, the wisdom that comes from practical experience.

Even an informal poll of experienced travelers will reveal a common opinion; it is very difficult to travel alone. Some might observe that it is even foolish. Still others may be even stronger in their opinion and go so far as to insist that it is necessary to have a guide, especially when you are traveling into uncharted waters and into territory that you have not yet experienced. I am of the personal opinion that a traveling companion is welcome under all circumstances. The thought of traveling alone, to some exciting destination without someone to share the journey with does not capture my imagination or channel my enthusiasm. However, with that being noted, what is simply a matter of preference on the normal journey becomes a matter of necessity when a person embarks on a spiritual journey.

The spiritual journey, which can be the most challenging of all journeys, is experienced best with a guide, a companion, or at the very least, a friend in whom you have placed your trust. This observation is not a preference or an opinion but rather an established spiritual necessity. All of the great saints with whom I am familiar had a spiritual director or a confessor who journeyed with them. Admittedly, at times the saint might well have traveled far beyond the experience of their guide and companion but more often than not they would return to their director and reflect on their experience. Understood in this sense, the director and companion provided a valuable contribution and necessary resource.

When I was learning how to pray (a necessity for anyone who desires to be a full-time and public "religious person"), the community of men that I belong to gave me a great gift. Between my second and third year in college, I was given a one-year sabbatical, with all expenses paid and all of my personal needs met. This period of time was called novitiate. I was officially designated as a novice, a beginner in the spiritual journey, and I was assigned a "master," a person who was willing to lead me. In addition to the master, I was provided with every imaginable book and any other resource that I could possibly need. Even with all that I was provided, I did not learn how to pray because of the books and the unlimited resources, rather it was the master, the companion who was the key to the experience.

One day, after about three months of reading, of quiet and solitude, and of practicing all of the methods and descriptions of prayer that were available to me, the master called. "Put away the books, forget the method, and just listen." We went into a room, became quiet, and tried to recall the presence of God, and then, the master simply prayed out loud and permitted me to listen to his prayer. As he prayed, he revealed his hopes, his dreams, his struggles, his successes, and most of all, his relationship with God. I discovered as I listened that his prayer was deeply intimate but most of all it was self-revealing. As I learned about him, I was led through his life experience to the place where God dwells. At that moment I was able to understand a little bit about what I was supposed to do if I really wanted to pray.

The dynamic of what happened when the master called, invited me to listen, and then revealed his innermost self to me as he communicated with God in prayer, was important. It wasn't so much that the master was trying to reveal to me what needed to be said; he was not inviting me to pray with the same words that he used, but rather that he was trying to bring me to that place within myself where prayer becomes possible. That place, a place of intimacy and of self-awareness, was a necessary stop on the journey and it was a place that I needed to be led to. I could not have easily discovered it on my own.

The purpose of the volume that you hold in your hand is to lead you, over a period of fifteen days or, maybe more realistically, fifteen prayer periods, to a place where prayer is possible. If you already have a regular experience and practice of prayer, perhaps this volume can help lead you to a deeper place, a more intimate relationship with the Lord.

It is important to note that the purpose of this book is not to lead you to a better relationship with Saint Bernard, your spiritual companion. Although your companion will invite you to share some of their deepest and most intimate thoughts, your companion is doing so only to bring you to that place where God dwells. After all, the true measurement of a companion for the journey is that they bring you to the place where you need to be, and then they step back, out of the picture. A guide who brings you to the desired destination and then sticks around is a very unwelcome guest!

Many times I have found myself attracted to a particular idea or method for accomplishing a task, only to discover that what seemed to be inviting and helpful possessed too many details. All of my energy went to the mastery of the details and I soon lost my enthusiasm. In each instance, the book that seemed so promising ended up on my bookshelf, gathering dust. I can assure you, it is not our intention that this book end up in your bookcase, filled with promise, but unable to deliver.

There are three simple rules that need to be followed in order to use this book with a measure of satisfaction.

Place: It is important that you choose a place for reading that provides the necessary atmosphere for reflection and that does not allow for too many distractions. Whatever place you choose needs to be comfortable, have the necessary lighting, and, finally, have a sense of "welcoming" about it. You need to be able to look forward to the experience of the journey. Don't travel steerage if you know you will be more comfortable in first class and if the choice is realistic for you. On the other hand, if first class is a distraction and you feel more comfortable and more yourself in steerage, then it is in steerage that you belong.

My favorite place is an overstuffed and comfortable chair in my bedroom. There is a light over my shoulder, and the chair reclines if I feel a need to recline. Once in a while, I get lucky and the sun comes through my window and bathes the entire room in light. I have other options and other places that are available to me but this is the place that I prefer.

Time: Choose a time during the day when you are most alert and when you are most receptive to reflection, meditation, and prayer. The time that you choose is an essential component. If you are a morning person, for example, you should choose a time that is in the morning. If you are more alert in the afternoon, choose an afternoon time slot; and if evening is your preference, then by all means choose the evening. Try to avoid "peak" periods in your daily routine when you know that you might be disturbed. The time that you choose needs to be your time and needs to work for you.

It is also important that you choose how much time you

will spend with your companion each day. For some it will be possible to set aside enough time in order to read and reflect on all the material that is offered for a given day. For others, it might not be possible to devote one time to the suggested material for the day, so the prayer period may need to be extended for two, three, or even more sessions. It is not important how long it takes you; it is only important that it works for you and that you remain committed to that which is possible.

For myself I have found that fifteen minutes in the early morning, while I am still in my robe and pajamas and before my morning coffee, and even before I prepare myself for the day, is the best time. No one expects to see me or to interact with me because I have not yet "announced" the fact that I am awake or even on the move. However, once someone hears me in the bathroom, then my window of opportunity is gone. It is therefore important to me that I use the time that I have identified when it is available to me.

Freedom: It may seem strange to suggest that freedom is the third necessary ingredient, but I have discovered that it is most important. By freedom I understand a certain "stance toward life," a "permission to be myself and to be gentle and understanding of who I am." I am constantly amazed at how the human person so easily sets himself or herself up for disappointment and perceived failure. We so easily make judgments about ourselves and our actions and our choices, and very often those judgments are negative, and not at all helpful.

For instance, what does it really matter if I have chosen a place and a time, and I have missed both the place and the time for three days in a row? What does it matter if I have chosen, in that twilight time before I am completely awake and still a little sleepy, to roll over and to sleep for fifteen minutes more? Does it mean that I am not serious about the journey, that I really don't want to pray, that I am just fooling myself when I say that my prayer time is important to me? Perhaps, but I prefer to believe that it simply means that I am tired and I just wanted a little more sleep. It doesn't mean anything more than that. However, if I make it mean more than that, then I can become discouraged, frustrated, and put myself into a state where I might more easily give up. "What's the use? I might as well forget all about it."

The same sense of freedom applies to the reading and the praying of this text. If I do not find the introduction to each day helpful, I don't need to read it. If I find the questions for reflection at the end of the appointed day repetitive, then I should choose to close the book and go my own way. Even if I discover that the reflection offered for the day is not the one that I prefer and that the one for the next day seems more inviting, then by all means, go on to the one for the next day.

That's it! If you apply these simple rules to your journey you should receive the maximum benefit and you will soon find yourself at your destination. But be prepared to be surprised. If you have never been on a spiritual journey you should know that the "travel brochures" and the other descriptions that you might have heard are nothing compared to the real thing. There is so much more than you can imagine.

A final prayer of blessing suggests itself:

Lord, catch me off guard today.
Surprise me with some moment of beauty
    or pain
So that at least for the moment
I may be startled into seeing that you are
    here in all your splendor,
Always and everywhere,
Barely hidden,
Beneath,
Beyond,
Within this life I breathe.

Frederick Buechner

REV. THOMAS M. SANTA, CSsR
LIGUORI, MISSOURI
FEAST OF THE PRESENTATION, 1999

A Brief Chronology
of the Life of Saint Bernard

1090: Bernard was born in 1090 in Fontaines (France), the third in a family of six sons and one daughter. His father was Tescelin Sorrel, the Lord of Fontaines, and his mother was Aleth of Montbard, both belonging to the highest nobility of Burgundy. His mother was a pious woman, dedicating all of her children to God at birth.

1099: Bernard was sent to a renowned secular school in Chatillon-sur-Seine; he was greatly fond of literature and poetry; his reasons were so that he could take up the study of sacred Scripture; he was an excellent student and seemed to be of remarkable virtue. It was said of him that "piety was his all"; he had a special devotion to the Blessed Virgin.

1109: Bernard's mother died, which had a tremendous effect upon him, throwing him into a state of prolonged and acute depression. During his youth, he was the subject of many temptations, but his virtue triumphed, often heroically; he often thought of retiring from the world to live a life of solitude and prayer.

1112: Bernard felt attached to the Benedictine monastery at Cîteaux, founded some fifteen years previously by Saint Robert. It is said that Bernard sought guidance for his future; kneeling in prayer at a wayside Church, he asked God's guidance. Upon arising, all of his doubts had vanished and he was resolved to follow the strict Cistercian way of life. Bernard, accompanied by thirty noblemen from Burgundy, sought admission to the order. It is notable that initially all of his brothers—with the exception of the youngest—accompanied him (later, his youngest brother, sister, and his father would join him).

From the start, Bernard trained himself to live by the order which he later gave to postulants: "If you desire to live in this house, leave your body behind; only spirits can enter here." At the end of that year, all of his companions, except one, made their profession and assumed the cloistered life.

1115: Saint Stephen, the Abbot of Cîteaux, sent Bernard, as the head of a group of twelve monks, to found a new Cistercian house at Vallée d'Absinthe (the valley of bitterness); Bernard named this Claire Vallée of Clairvaux (June 25, 1115)—the names Bernard and Clairvaux, from then on, became synonymous; Bernard was named the abbot.

Clairvaux appeared to be a desolate place. Bernard once said: "Our fathers built their monasteries in damp, unwholesome places, so that the monks might have the uncertainty of life more sharply before their eyes." They had, in fact, chosen swampy land, which they rapidly transformed into fertile fields through their diligence. The austerities were severe and Bernard's health suffered; he was forced to mitigate the austerities at the urging of his friend, William, the bishop of Champeaux. Bernard became very popular and people flocked in by the hundreds to join and follow the order under his direction. Soon, the monastery became too small for all of the religious there.

1118: Bernard suffered greatly from stomach problems, but he never complained; his life was in danger—his friend, William, asked and received orders from the Cistercian chapter to relieve Bernard of his duties for twelve months; knowing that Bernard required rest and quiet in order to regain his health, William placed Bernard in a hermitage, with orders that he not follow the rule and free his mind from all of the concerns of the community. Bernard lived there, under a doctor's care, following a special diet, and returned to the monastery in improved health.

1119: Bernard was present at the first general chapter held by the order; not yet thirty, he was listened to with great attention and respect. In this Chapter, the constitution of the Order was written as well as the regulations of the "Charter of Charity," which was confirmed by Pope Callixtus on December 23, 1119.

1120: Bernard composed his first work: "De Gradibus Superbiae et Humilitatis" as well as his Homilies (sermons). There was opposition to his rules by the "Black Monks" and Bernard's response was entitled, "The Apology," which was divided into two parts: his proof of innocence and his reasons for his attacks on previous severe abuses by the clergy. He also wrote "Grace and Free Will" around this same time.

1121: Bernard performed his first miracle. While saying Mass, he restored speech to a mute man, enabling him to make his final confession before his death, three days later. There are also numerous accounts of sick people being cured by Bernard simply making the Sign of the Cross over them—this attested to by eyewitness accounts.

1122: Bernard continued to experience poor health and was taken from manual labor and directed to devote himself to preaching and writing. He wrote his Treatise on "Degrees of Humility and Pride," which contains an admirable analysis of the human character. Bernard preached at the University and gained many candidates for holy orders. Erasmus is quoted as saying: "Bernard is an eloquent preacher, much more by nature than art; he is full of charm and vivacity and knows how to reach and move the affections."

1123–1127:

Bernard, in spite of his longing for a cloistered life, traveled Europe on missions connected with the Church. His reputation for learning and sanctity as well as his talents as a mediator became so famous that we was called upon by princes, bishops, and popes for his advice. Bernard is quoted as saying about this period: "my life is overrun everywhere by anxieties, suspicions, and cares. There is scarcely an hour free from the crowd of discordant applicants, and the troubles and cares of their businesses. I have no power to stop their coming and cannot refuse to see them, and they do not leave me even time to pray."

1128: Bernard assisted in the Council of Troyes, the purpose of which was to settle certain disputes of the bishops of Paris; he was appointed secretary and given the task of drawing up the synodal statutes. His outspoken censures had their effect on changing the way of life of several clergy; many gave up their secular holdings, positions, and wealth, returning to a more austere lifestyle.

Bernard drafted the outline of the Rule of the Knights Templar at this council.

1130: Pope Honorius II died (February 14) and a schism in the Church developed as the result of the election of two popes—Innocent II (by the majority) and Anacletus II, who succeeded in getting the strongholds of Rome into his hands; Innocent fled to Pisa. A Council was soon held, Bernard attended (chosen to judge between the two rivals) and, as a result of his vigorous defence, Innocent was recognized, calming the country's troubles, reconciling all factions.

1132–1133:

Innocent visited Bernard and Bernard accompanied him to Italy; the pope abolished the dues Clairvaux had to pay.

1134–1138:

Another schism was squelched by Bernard; Bernard continued throughout Europe as a mediator for religious matters. At this time, he wrote his *Sermon on the Canticle of Canticles*. Anacletus died "of grief and disappointment" in 1138, as did the schism; it was then voted to excommunicate schismatics.

1139–1142:

Bernard assisted in the Second General Lateran Council and in the Tenth Ecumenical, at which the surviving adherents of the schism were definitively condemned.

Bernard was visited by Saint Malachy (a zealous reformer of monasticism), metropolitan of the Church in Ireland, who became a very close friend (and later died in Clairvaux in 1148).

Bernard resumed his lectures and was denounced as a heretic (he was found innocent) regarding his opinions on Abelard's views—Abelard was later formally arraigned on a number of accounts of heresy—and was condemned on seventeen counts, sentencing him to silence. (He died as a result of a breakdown in 1142.) Bernard was severely criticized for his uncompromising attitude, but he stated that Abelard's brilliance made him extremely dangerous.

1143: Innocent II died; one of Bernard's disciples, Bernard of Pisa (later known as Eugenius III), became the pope. At his request, Bernard sent him various instructions which make up the "Book of Consideration"—the main focus of which is that the reformation of the Church should begin with the sanctity of the head. Temporal matters are merely accessories; the main ones are piety and meditation (or consideration), which must precede action. This book contains some of the most beautiful writings about the papacy, and has always been treasured by the sovereign popes, many of whom used it for their ordinary reading.

1144–1146:

Bernard was commissioned by the pope to preach a new Crusade; many miracles were witnessed, which undoubtedly contributed to its success.

1147–1152:

The Second Crusade was a failure; many people were led by sordid motives, committing lawless acts along the march. Bernard was severely criticized as he had promised success. In reply, he declared that he had trusted Divine Mercy to bless the Crusade undertaken for the honor of His Name, but that the army's sins had brought upon the catastrophe, stating: "How is it that the rashness of mortals dares condemn what they cannot understand?"

1153: During the last years of his life, Bernard was greatly saddened by the failure of the Crusade he had preached—assuming the entire responsibility for its failure.

From the beginning of 1153, Bernard felt his death approaching. Pope Eugenius died, robbing him of his closest friend and supporter. Bernard stated: "The saints were moved to pray for death out of a longing to see Christ, but I am driven hence by scandals and evil." Bernard died at the age of 63 on August 20th, after having been an abbot for 38 years (in the cloister for 40), personally founding over 160 monasteries in various parts of Europe. (At the time of his death, they numbered over 400.) He was the first Cistercian monk placed on the calendar of Saints and was canonized by Pope Alexander III on January 18, 1174. Pope Pius bestowed the title of Doctor of the Church on him in 1830. His relics are at Clairvaux, his skull in the Cathedral in Troyes; his emblems are a pen, bees, and instruments of the passion. His feast day is August 20.

Saint Bernard exerted a great influence on monasticism: he encouraged monks to devote themselves to mystical prayer in the regular framework of monastic observance; and he modified the concepts of early Cîteaux in practice, developing the Cistercian order.

Introduction

IN HIS *SERMONS FOR THE YEAR*, one theme keeps reappearing to their author which is central and very important to him: the conversion of this desire which dwells in us and constitutes what we are. In other words, how can we bring all of the parts of what we are, which we are tempted to distrust (affectivity, feelings), into the dynamism of the spiritual life, when we naively confuse it with faith? To Bernard, faith is something else. But our affectivity is urgently invited to enter into the movement of faith in order to become fervor, a spark and love, so that faith, instead of remaining only cerebral, also seizes our desire and makes it the force of our will.

This theme (the conversion of desire) appears interesting to us, so useful to study more deeply that we have decided to retain it as the central theme of this book. We have chosen many of Bernard's texts from his *Sermons for the Year* and ask you to please pardon their limiting choice, however its great advantage is the obvious unity of this book through the diversity of its chapters.

Another theme serves to frame the book, since it characterizes the first and last chapters (days), reappearing again in the eleventh: humility, one of the great focal points of Bernard's works—humility as a means of gratitude and choice of the true grandeur, first in God, as well as in Mary, and then in ourselves.

It is to indicate the climate of holiness, but also of the health in what is the most objective in us, our understanding, and what is the most subjective in us, our affectivity, which must let themselves be motivated by faith. That is how this could become the truth for us, on the one hand, and spiritual willingness on the other.

We will then follow the directions of this path of conversion of our subjectivity through the diverse aspects of Christian life: listening to God's word, the prayer of supplication and thanksgiving, the experience of suffering, fraternal love, the perspective of death and eternal life.

Recapitulatory chapters are not found at the end of this book, but in the middle: it is through our desire itself, which becomes a search for God, that God finds us and we find him within ourselves. The spark for our search depends upon our experience with the presence of God. What a requirement...yes, don't be discouraged, for God does not ask for us to have already arrived, but that we constantly continue the journey; our holiness is a work in progress.

15 Days of Prayer
With Saint Bernard

DAY ONE

Christmas: God's Humility, a Model for Our Own

FOCUS POINT

If God, who is greater than all measure, when he became in-
carnate in the person of Jesus Christ, lived his earthly life in a
state of humility and loving service, how then shall we choose
to live our lives? When faced with the humble sacrifice of our
Creator, how can we live our lives with any pretense of being
greater than anyone else? There is a link with the divine in the
manner of humility, and as servants of God we must not stray
from its path. We must pray for the grace of God to fill us with
the desire to serve humbly, as he did.

*Truly, my friends, the feast day of the birth of the Lord, which
we celebrate today, is a great one. But the day is short, so we
must abbreviate the sermon. It is not a surprise that we make
our talk brief since God the Father, himself, made it so that his
own Word-made-flesh would be with us only briefly. Would
you like to know just what greatness he attained and to what
brevity he was brought? "Do I not fill heaven and earth? says
the Lord" (Jer 23:24). Yet now, the Word became flesh (Jn
1:14) and he was laid in a manger (Lk 2:7). Even at the age of
just one day, the prophet told us: "From everlasting to everlasting you are God" (Ps 90:2).*

*Why, brothers? What need pushed the Lord of majesty to
empty himself in this way (Phil 2:7ff), to humble himself, and
to make his existence brief, if not to set an example for you so
that you do as he had done (Jn 13:15)? His example shouted
this to us and then his words proclaimed: "Learn from me, for
I am gentle and humble in heart" (Mt 11:29).*[1]

E verything begins with an astonishment. Everything: faith,
a Christian life, the action of repentance, spiritual reflection, prayer, and feelings for someone else.

An astonishment that is constantly renewed. An astonishment to see that God always takes the initiative to come to us,
like he did at Christmas.

In his youth, around the age of twelve, Saint Bernard had
an exceptional interior experience at Christmastime. It was an
experience that definitively determined his conception of God
and human life. He had a vision that, for an instant, showed
him the Blessed Virgin breast-feeding her child. The God of
majesty came all the way to him—all the way into him—

through this small child: God's Word-made-flesh, in his immensity and creative powerfulness, shortened and concentrated into this newborn baby, the divine glory, hidden and revealed into that which is the humblest of beings here on earth: a baby in the arms of his mother.

It was a radical astonishment which Bernard never recovered from, an astonishment which changed into a marvel for him—and for us. It is the very image of God, the image that we spontaneously have, that absolutely changes: a God whose grandeur is overbearing, overwhelming, and arrogant. (We come back to this model of grandeur, more or less of our own making, all the while doubting it.) And a God that is remote, a stranger, which we must try to make interested in us in order to make him favorable and, if possible, useful.

But if this child, born during a trip, in a stable, laid in a manger, wrapped in swaddling clothes, who suckles and warms up a young woman, who is poor and underprivileged, much like today's refugees—yes, if this child is God, the Son of God, doesn't our very idea of grandeur and humility change completely? And then so does the image that we have of God.

We think that we know everything yet we must relearn everything by contemplating the Christmas child.

Are grandeur and smallness less incompatible than we thought? Is humility another thing altogether, rather than the sad humiliation to which we almost inevitably identify it? Is it something other than the types of past experiences which have hurt us: feelings of failure, of not measuring up, the haunting memory of being abandoned, the fear of being scorned, the necessity of putting ourselves down in order to be accepted....

Bernard asked: "What need pushed the Lord of majesty to empty himself in this way?" And his answer: "to set an example for you so that you do as he had done." In other words, no other need than the one of revealing our human truth to us. And then the Lord's truth to himself. A need that is his very freedom, his sovereignty. Yes: God's humility, the birth of the Lord into our life—even more than this: through the destitution of a poor child—that is the only meaning for this world, the only truth for these times, of God's eternal, heavenly grandeur. For his grandeur is his mercy and mercy could be nothing but humble.

> But he emptied himself of that which concerned his power and majesty, but not of his goodness and mercy. What does the apostle Paul say about this? "But the goodness and kindness of God our Savior appeared" (Titus 3:4). His power, beforehand, had revealed itself through the creation of beings, and his wisdom through governing them. But now his goodness and mercy are most fully manifested in his humility. (...)
>
> May mercy then push beyond its limits, lengthen its cords (Isa 54:2), so that it enlarges its reach, so that it reaches mightily from one end of the earth to the other (Wis 8:1). Lord, your heart is laced by judgment: unbuckle your belt and come, overflowing with mercy and cascading with charity!

In effect, we come to the conclusion that the Lord's mercy is not a sign of weakness or inaction. His holiness, his requirements, and his "judgment" are all part of him and of the way we love him. But if his mercy is not a sign of weakness, the holiness of his judgment is not an indication of the inflexibility, restriction, or limitations inflicted on his love, but like Bernard says here, an overflowing of mercy, a cascade of charity.

That is the marvel.

The first consequence for us is this: the Lord's approach is good news, not a cause for fear, a desire to flee, or a need to hide.

> "The voice is heard…in our land" (Song 2:12): the Lord arrives! "Where can I go from your spirit? Where can I flee from your presence?" (Ps 139:7). No, don't be afraid, don't flee. He does not come armed, he does not come to punish, but to save. And so that you will not now say to him: "I heard the sound of you…and I hid myself" (Gen 3:10), here is the child, one without a voice. For the cries of a newborn provoke tenderness rather than fear. Yet if they frighten someone, it will not be you.
>
> Yes, he became a small child: the Blessed Virgin, his mother, wrapped him in bands of cloth (Lk 2:7), and you shake with fear (Ps 13:4)? At least, from this sign, you will know that he came to save you, not to lose you, to deliver you, not to bind you. Christ, the power of God and the wisdom of God (1 Cor 1:24) already goes to battle against your enemies, he already treads on their backs (Deut 33:29).

Certainly, great power is hidden in this weakness, there is great strength in humility: precisely, through love. And violence is truly unleashed, a battle begins. Not against us, but just the opposite, for us. Against the force of death which circles us from outside and eats away at us from within. God-made-man made himself my ally against my enemies. Will I not make myself become his ally against them?

Two enemies line themselves up against you: sin and death, in other words, the death of both the body and the soul. He comes to make them retreat, he will save you from both: do not be afraid. In truth, he had already vanquished sin in his own person when he assumed a human nature without the least contamination. In effect, the violence that was inflicted against sin was great and, we can be sure that it had been truly chased away when our nature, glorified to have been totally invaded and occupied, finds itself to be in Christ, absolutely disengaged from its possession.

Since then, Christ pursues your enemies, identifies them, and does not return until they are consumed (Ps 18:37). By fighting sin through his behavior, he attacks it through his words and example. But it is by his passion that he ties it up—yes, he ties it up and plunders its property (see Mt 12:29).

The second consequence of our marvel when faced with God's humility is that we discover our own humility there as our own most personal truth.

This is truly why I implore you, brothers, and I multiply my efforts: don't endure this most precious model shown to you in vain, but conform to he who renews the spirit of your minds (Eph 4:23). Strive for humility for it is the foundation and the guardian of all virtues; follow it closely, for it alone has the power to save your souls (Jas 1:21).

What could be more unseemly, abominable, and more seriously punishable for a man than to see the God of heaven turn himself into a small child, while he continues to make himself greater above the earth? What unbearable impudence, while the Majesty empties himself, if the small earthworm swells with his own importance!

Yes, the humility that Jesus reveals to us and the one to which we are called, simply consists of renouncing the illusion. This pretense of filling the voids that are within ourselves and denying our limitations is useless and vain. We must present them to God as if they are free space that he will fill with his life.

This pride that consists of disposing of everything around us and bringing everything to ourselves is useless and vain, for we are not the center. Must we say that God is the center? More exactly, the center is his covenant, through which he calls us to him, because then, in it, he comes to us.

This need to give ourselves value, as if we have been our own source, is useless and vain. We are only ourselves as a result of what we receive from God and what we offer of ourselves to him in response to the gift that he made to us of himself. God's law is the law of giving.

Like the image of God, our humility will be like an increase of confidence and interior freedom and a dimension of love. Then the fruit of astonishment and marvel will be constantly renewed.

Let us contemplate at length about Jesus, God's humility. Let us then ask ourselves about our own. And may this interrogation quickly turn us towards God through prayer where we will learn to be from him, like him, gentle and humble in heart.

REFLECTION QUESTIONS

In what ways can I become more humble in my own life? What tasks can I engage in that will help to develop my humility? Can I pray that, before I enter into any kind of service or ministry, I will reflect on the state of humility to which I am called by God in this capacity? How might reading Scripture daily assist me, teaching me what it means to be truly humble?

DAY TWO

Christmas and the Ascension: The Conversion of Understanding and Desire

FOCUS POINT

Faith and understanding are not meant to be separated. In fact, Jesus came to us that we might understand. Yes, we must have faith, since there are mysteries we cannot understand, but it is always *faith seeking understanding*. In light of the revelation that Jesus has imparted, we must direct our desire toward the singular goal of knowing and understanding everything in the light of Jesus, the way, the truth, and the life.

*There are two parts of ourselves, then, understanding and de-
sire, that must be purified: the understanding, so that it may
know; and the desire, so that it may will. (...)*

*Our understanding was disordered, not to say blinded; (our)
desire was tainted, and very tainted. But Christ enlightens our
understanding, (and) the Holy Spirit purifies our desire.2*

T his way of presenting the interior man may actually serve
our needs well. In fact, within us, there is a more objective faculty (reason, understanding) that intends to reach ex-
terior objects in their own reality. And, there is also a more
subjective dimension within us (order, feelings, affectivity, spark
of desire). This encompasses all of the reactions of the person
we are with respect to what will affect us from within, or from
outside of ourselves.

Is it certain that we don't put understanding and faith in
opposition? Is it certain that, for us, the healthy exercise of
reason does not always demand that we put our faith aside?
(That is the method of the exact sciences.) In other respects,
doesn't faith seem to presuppose a certain retreat from understanding? And from the viewpoint of this one, the admission
of incompetence? Then, the question virtually asks itself: in
order to adhere to Christ and the gospel, must we sacrifice the
unity of our person, in particular, the use of our capacity to
reflect and understand?

In other respects, what becomes of our sensitivities, our
subjective reactions in the spiritual adventure of faith? The
problem is actually posed with a certain acuity. Some people,
naively and voluntarily intermingle faith with what they feel.
In fact, they replace faith with feeling, in this way becoming,

themselves, the norm of truth, the thermometer of their fervor, the yardstick of the qualities of their prayer and love, the barometer of their spiritual progress. From others, by denouncing that with reason, and knowing that faith is on the outside of feelings and our subjective reactions, then not knowing what to do about these feelings or reactions: by means of mistrusting them, they practically exclude them from the spiritual life. Very true, but without them, are we still ourselves?

Today, there are infinitely more problems than intellectual ones. For over three hundred years, true difficulties have inhibited the progress of Christians. With Saint Bernard, the advantage is that he approaches these questions in a very different manner and proposes welcome solutions to us. To sum it up, he conceives of faith as a conversion of understanding and desire.

For the Son of God came. He worked so many great and wondrous deeds in the world, that with good cause, he called our understanding away from all worldly matters. Thus, we could ponder, and never have enough of pondering, that he has done wondrous deeds (Ps 98:1). Truly, he left very extensive fields for our discerning to roam, and the river of these ponderings is so very deep, that, in the words of the Prophet, it cannot be crossed (Ezek 47:5). Who can sufficiently ponder how the Lord has come before us, come to us, come to our assistance; and how his unparalleled Majesty willed to die so that we might live, to serve so that we might reign, to live in exile so that we might be brought home again, and even to stoop to the most menial actions so as to give us (see Gen 41:41) all his works.

The Lord of the apostles presented himself to the

apostles in such a way that they would no longer perceive the invisible things of God as understood by the
things that are made (Rom 1:20), but that the very
Maker of all things would himself be seen face to face
(1 Cor 13:12).

Does it not seem to you that he enlightened their
understanding when he opened their mind(s) to the
understanding of the Scriptures, making known that
Christ had to suffer these things and rise from the dead,
and so enter into his glory (Lk 24:25–27; 45–46)?

For understanding, to convert is not to scuttle oneself, nor to
change our nature, but to allow oneself to be visited by Christ,
illuminated by his gospel, and seized by God's truth. That is
Bernard's conception (and those of his era). On the one hand,
faith is an intensive quality within us, a recognition. In it, it
calls to our understanding: to our faculty to receive a teaching,
to perceive its meaning, to organize the knowledge, to assimilate it, and to adapt it to ourselves. On the condition that we
don't exaggerate the critical role of reason, elevate mistrust to
a level of supreme value, reason or understanding is truly the
place within us where God's Word comes to echo and where it
could receive our adhesion. In this case—like each time that it
is used with reference to people and not things—our understanding estimates, by reflection, that it could have good reasons to trust the person who is speaking and to offer him a
welcome, be receptive, pay attention and understand.

If the Son of God was united with us at Christmas, and
during his entire life on earth, it was (Bernard tells us) in order
to allow the apostles—and us through their teachings—to have
access to God's truth, the revelation of his project of alliance.
In this order of realities which fail our senses, in this order

where the present world has no meaning, except with respect to changes to come, man's spirit, reduced to its own capacities, doesn't go very far. He must be illuminated and in order for this to happen, he must encounter the very light of God and his Word. But it must be a light that is adapted to the possibilities of our understanding, a Word that is translated into man's language, a presence of God that becomes human around us.

It was necessary, then, for the Son of God to come to us as Jesus of Nazareth so that our understanding could turn itself to him and welcome him. Thus, our understanding is called to make a conversion, more and more towards him, and to then reach its highest level of capacity. It is not at all necessary to be very knowledgeable or intellectual to become a Christian. But it is necessary for us—and it is a grace and an honor—to commit all of our capacities of understanding to the service of faith.

Still, having grown accustomed to that most holy flesh of his, they could not listen to a word about his departure: that the one for whom they had left everything (Mt 19:27) would leave them. What is the reason for this? Their understanding was enlightened, but their desire was not yet "purified" whence their kind Teacher gently and tenderly addressed them, saying: "It is to your advantage that I go away, for if I do not go away, the Advocate will not come to you" (Jn 16:7). "But because I have said these things to you, sorrow has filled your hearts" (Jn 16:6).

And as they wept (Jn 16:20), Christ was lifted up to heaven (Lk 24:51; Acts 1:9). He sent the Holy Spirit (Acts 2:2), who purified their desire, that is, their will; or rather he transformed it, so that those who, at first, wanted to detain the Lord, now preferred that he ascend. What he had foretold to them was fulfilled: "You will weep and mourn, but the world will rejoice; you will have pain, but your pain will turn into joy" (Jn 16:20). In this way then, their discerning was enlightened by Christ, and their will purified by the Spirit, so that just as they knew the good, they also willed it. This alone is perfect religion and religious perfection (see Jas 1:27).

At the other end of Jesus' earthly life was the Ascension, when he entered into this new existence, in this way, escaping from our sight, our feelings, and our present and concrete experience. In a manner that is original and striking, Bernard explains to us that this departure, this absence, was also as necessary for our emotions as the Incarnation was for our understanding.

It is a fact: even before (and in view of) being able to know, the human being has desires, the desire for happiness and plenitude. More precisely, at the beginning, at the very least, he is infinite in his desires (plural), in the aspect of being, to always be more and always better. That is the dynamism that makes him live. But the double-edged sword that terribly threatens desire is, on the one hand, that we are avowedly egocentric ("me, nothing but me, everything for me") and, on the other hand, we thrown ourselves completely towards the goal of the most immediate satisfaction ("everything, right now"). It is a failure in both cases, because dynamism, instead of bringing us far along, lasts a long time. We must unravel our desire so that instead of turning against us, it brings us beyond our limits; and it is necessary to unify it into a single bundle which, beyond the urgency of things and the world, aims at what we are called to become. The goal to which we confusedly aspire is neither within ourselves, nor in immediate satisfaction.

Bernard rightly notes: the apostles, having known to recognize Jesus through their understanding, had only one desire in their understanding: to keep him with them and for them, in this world and this life. But it is to something else that God destines us: to this new world and to this new future to which Jesus has come to open our spirit, to this new world and to this future where he was arisen and to which the Holy Spirit, already so very imperceptible, is already bursting. Our desire is thus called to convert itself. Are we called to abandon ourselves as being unworthy of God? Certainly not. Are we called to renounce numerous things and pleasures that seem to collide? Yes, but to do it in order to advance this quest of pleasure, this taste of happiness, this appetite of totality which is building towards Christ. We have often learned to oppose desire and will, pleasure and want, taste and need. And will no longer appears like a constraint, a state of tension, forbidden, or repression. In fact, Bernard was right: the will was nothing more that the spark of desire, once it is organized with a goal in sight which convinces it and seizes it. However it is precisely this goal that faith proposes to it so that it deploys all of its dynamism in it, so that it will go all the way to the end of itself and receive its progressive unity from it.

By entering into this process of conversion, it will finally find its truth, the spark of desire, with the affective strengths it brings along with it and the feelings which echo in it—Bernard calls it "fervor." Bernard did not conceive of us serving God without wanting to, without warmth, happiness, or enthusiasm. But how? Under what conditions? That is what we will see in the following chapters. For Bernard never stopped coming back to the way of realizing this conversion of our desire.

For now, our meditation and prayer could be based on the following themes:

—Christmas: Jesus came to us in order to open the understanding of our faith to his light;
—The Ascension: Jesus visibly left us in order to bring the affective desire of our faith with him;
—Our spiritual life is not an abandonment, but a conversion of all our intellectual and affective powers;
—Our interior unity is realized through this movement by which the desire strives to join our understanding, and through the renewal of our fervor, which the understanding receives from the spark of desire.

REFLECTION QUESTIONS

Do I separate faith and understanding in my life? Or do I desire to unite the two? Is my faith seeking understanding? Do I attempt to view the world—to understand the universe around me—in light of the revelation of Jesus Christ? How does the revelation of Jesus Christ affect my relationship with the people I encounter, with the books and articles I read, with the choices I make concerning the environment? How do I unite the decisions I make in my life to my desire to understand Jesus in the light of faith?

DAY THREE

Assimilate the Word of God

FOCUS POINT

Living the Word of God means just that—*living* the Word of God. Scripture can be committed to memory and lost. And what does it benefit a person to be able to quote Scripture when that person does not apply those words to his or her own life? The Word of God must be internalized like food—after all, it is manna from heaven—so that it becomes the very essence of our person, and exudes from us, in our words and actions effortlessly, without our mind or our pride aware of the good we are doing living by the Word of God.

So that you may not suppose that what I say [of this second coming] is an invention of my own; listen to His own words: "Those who love me will keep my word, and my Father will love them, and we will come to them and make our home with them" (Jn 14:23). But what does he mean by these words? For I read elsewhere: "Whoever fears the Lord will do this" (Sir 15:1): but I think that something more is said of him who loves God, that is, that he will keep the words of God. But where are they to be kept? In the heart, without doubt, as the Prophet says: "I treasure your word in my heart, so that I may not sin against you" (Ps 119:11). But how are they to be preserved in the heart? Or is it sufficient to preserve them only in the memory? But the Apostle says to those who preserve them in this way: "Knowledge puffs up" (1 Cor 8:1). And besides, that which is committed only to the memory is easily forgotten (Sermons for Advent).

▬▬▬▬▬

Must we, once again, repeat what we know? Must we repeat that God's Word was not given just for us to hear, but for us to put into practice? Didn't Jesus teach us: "it was not those who said: Lord, Lord..."? Why repeat it then?—Not because we would ignore it, but there is always the chance that we may forget. And because, even by striving, we will never totally attain it, above all, not definitively. We must constantly apply ourselves to it, constantly break out of our feelings of discouragement, lethargy, and habits in order to regain the attention, imagination, and strength without which we once again neglect to put what we expect into perspective with what we must live.

We are not amazed then that Saint Bernard also speaks about it. But we notice that he was not satisfied just to repeat the admonishment. He was more closely interested in the type of welcome the Word of God requires from us in order to have the opportunity to become alive.

One day, during Advent, before his listeners, he evoked a theme that he kept close to his heart: it was an original and personal idea, for which he knew no precursors. Bernard noted that between the two comings (advents) of Christ, which are well known to Christians, the first being his birth in Bethlehem, the second when he will establish his Kingdom, there is a third. Yes, a third advent, or rather an intermediate advent where Jesus is now with us "in the Spirit and power," to be our comfort, which makes us progress from the first to the last advent.

But then Bernard had a crisis of conscience: on what did he base his idea? He answered:

We ought then to keep the Word of God (Jn 8:51) in the same way as we are able to keep the food of the body, and we can do this more easily, as that Word itself is "the bread that came down from heaven" (Jn 6:41), the food of the soul. Earthly bread, while it is still in the cupboard, may be stolen by a thief, gnawed by mice or corrupted by age. But when you have eaten it, you don't need to fear any of these dangers. Keep the Word of God in this same way: "Blessed rather are those who hear the Word of God and obey it" (Lk 11:28). Let it be deposited in the innermost parts of your soul, let it pass into your affections and into your character. Feed upon this good food to the fullest, and your soul shall delight itself in its feast. Do not forget to feed upon this bread so that your heart will not become withered (Ps 102:5); but let your soul be filled with its feast (Ps 63:5).

If you keep the Word of God in this way, without a doubt, you will be kept by it. For the Son will come to you with the Father (Jn 14:23); that great Prophet (Lk

7:16) will come who will rebuild Jerusalem and make
all things new (Rev 21:5).[3]

In this passage, we can recognize the major themes of the last
chapter: understanding, which includes memory and the spark
of desire, but here, with reference to the "innermost parts of
the soul," there, where it "delights in its feast" and with reference also to the "heart" which must not "become withered,"
and finally, with the way in which we live.

Further, in the quotation at the beginning of this chapter,
Bernard made a distinction between, on the one hand, Sirach's
adage: "Whoever fears the Lord will do this" (where it is understood that what is good is revealed to us by God, and where
it is affirmed that we must put the will of God into practice),
and on the other hand, Jesus' words which are a promise rather
than an admonishment: "Those who love me will keep my
word...."

It is a subtle distinction, but an important one. The two
phrases aim at the same goal (to concretely live the Word), but
Jesus' phrase said much more by speaking about "love" and
"keep." Between hearing, which keeps the Word in our understanding, and the putting of it into practice, there is, according
to what Bernard says here, a necessity for this word to enter
the heart, where it will be "kept."

Our intellectual attention will tend to receive God's Word
in the heart like information and, should the case arise, like an
order that it will store in the memory, then, if everything goes
well, it will be transformed into concrete actions. But then
Christian faith follows on the path of pure moralism. A good
practice, yes, but one which runs the risk of becoming a goal
in itself (to do good because it is good), and turning into pride
("puffed up"). It is a practice which will inevitably lose its

steam and where the heart will wither—a practice without mysticism.

"To keep" his word when we act on the words of Jesus whom we love, is something other than to memorize them, Bernard tells us. It is here that we must unite the attention of our understanding with the effort of our memory and our subjectivity in order to relay and deepen them. Yes, we have the capacity within ourselves to be touched, to find beauty, to be enthused, to affectively attach ourselves; the capacity to vividly feel and strongly vibrate.

Certainly, we could remain where we are in superficial sentimentalism, or seek feelings for their own sake. We could only vibrate with that which comes to our most easy pleasure. Bernard tells us that it doesn't stop: it is through this dimension of our affectivity, by engaging the force of our desire and capacity for pleasure that we must interiorize God's Word all the way to the depths of our being—our heart, and the innermost depth of our soul. And similarly, it is by vibrating to this Word, by allowing it to seize our feelings, by joining it with the strength of our feelings, that, beyond it, our love will go to Christ who told this to us—even more, to Christ who, through it, comes to live in us with the Father, through the Holy Spirit.

We see that, without understanding and memory, the heart will not recognize Christ in his words. But, without the heart, the understanding will limit itself to one understanding: left to itself, it could only peel away biblical passages by cutting them away from the One who is speaking. What we have called mystical above, is this assimilation where, on the one hand, Christ himself is loved and received through his words, and, on the other hand, his words dwell within us as if "your soul is filled with its feast," like a food that gives life, a force that remains alive, a generous grace. Then their practice—indispensable, certainly—will not be the goal by an overflow of the mystery and the test of its authenticity. We must reread the last paragraph of Bernard's text that is cited above: if we mobilize all our strength to keep the Word of God in this way, we will be kept by it, and all things will be made new in us. This comment is important. To act in the name of faith is to let it happen. To keep is to be kept. We have noted that Christian practices quickly run dry: what a weakening of will occurs between the initiation of our projects and their completion! There is quite a difference between our intentions and our concrete attitudes! What can we do? Do we become discouraged? Or do we make the best of this mediocrity? In order to support the inevitable relativity of our practices, without being resigned to them, it is necessary for our absolute to be elsewhere, like a mystery, a source which dwells within us, but which doesn't belong to us. That will be Christ, the one who keeps us and renews us, thanks to his words which we keep.

Where is prayer in all of this? It is the very avenue and the occasion where, by affectivity, God's Word descends from the understanding to the heart. Bernard tells us that this assimilation is not automatic. No, it is not evident at all that this affectivity, the spark of desire, and the force of pleasure stretches themselves towards God's Word in order to assimilate it—and above all, to allow it to conquer them. Alas, it is very possible for us to hear this word absent-mindedly when our desires wander elsewhere....

It is through meditation that understanding, after being concentrated on that which has been read or heard, invites the feelings to unite with it more widely. And the spark of desire must make itself become a prayer within ourselves in order to be able to assimilate God's Word, like spiritual food which gives us life.

Bernard did not specifically speak of the Eucharist here, but the Word and the Sacrament are one and the same, like a spiritual assimilation, and, through it, we welcome the living Christ into ourselves. The word tells us what we receive in the Eucharist, and the eucharistic feast lets us feel, physically and spiritually, what Christ tells us.

REFLECTION QUESTIONS

How do I assimilate the Word of God into my own life? Do I meditate on that Word and absorb it into my life so that I live the Word without my pride entering in? Do I consume the Word as I consume the Eucharist, so that it is internalized and made an integral part of my person, more so than if it were merely committed to memory? Do I live the Word? Does the Word exude from my personality; is it a natural expression of who I am?

DAY FOUR

The Qualities of Prayer

FOCUS POINT
There are perils that face us in prayer. Prayer that is too timid, too self-assured, or too lukewarm is to be avoided. Reliance on God's mercy is the key. God knows what we need, what is good for us. More than petitioning God's grace, more than demanding what we think we need, what is necessary is trust. When we pray, we must trust in God's generosity. We must have faith that God—in his great mercy—will provide us what he sees fit for our spiritual well-being.

The more that prayer is active, if it is practiced like it should be, the more the Enemy habitually shows himself able to make himself an obstacle.

In fact, it happens that prayer runs into a lack of spiritual

*courage and excessive fear. And this happens regularly when
man is too conscious of his own indignity that he stops turning his eyes towards God's goodness. However, "Deep calls to
deep" (Ps 42:7): the depths of light to the depths of darkness,
the depths of mercy to that of misery. In fact, the heart of man
is deep and unfathomable. But if my uncertainty is great, Lord,
your goodness is even greater. Also, when my soul is troubled
for its own sake (Ps 6:4), I remember the intensity of your
mercy (Ps 106:7), and I gain strength from it; and when I come
to consider my abilities, I do not only want to remember your
righteousness (see Ps 71:16).*[4]

D o we recognize ourselves in the phrase "excessive fear,"
in this feeling of guilt and indignity that paralyzes both
our psychological and spiritual life, in this impression of failure, in the intimate parts of our self, which even removes our
confidence in God and keeps our outlook riveted on ourself?
Is that humility? Certainly not. It is a mixture of humiliation
and endemic depression in which we close ourselves off. And
in this case, will prayer be something other than a weak mum-
bling with no conviction?

The answer that Bernard addresses to such people is a
marvel of understanding and righteous in tone. It is useless to
stir up the depressives and to call upon their will: that is what
is ill and appears cornered. Bernard cites a fragment of a psalm
which suddenly takes on an unsuspected meaning: "Deep calls
to deep." Must we understand that if we feel a depth of nothingness, we must call upon the immense mercy of God? That
would be too voluntary. It is something altogether different
that Bernard proclaims: if you feel a depth of shadow and mis-

ery, know that this depth is precisely God—the depth of light and mercy—calling to this great void which you feel within yourself. At the beginning, nothing is asked of you than to believe that God's generosity is infinitely broader and deeper than your misery. And to know that God holds you more dear than you hold him.

He then said: "I do not only want to remember your righteousness." That means that God, instead of appearing to you to exact requirements and strict justice, appears to you through his goodness and mercy. However, as Saint John wrote, "God is greater than our hearts" (1 Jn 3:20).

Take a deep breath, lift up your eyes towards God's goodness. May your prayer find strength and confidence in it, through this assurance he gives you: he calls you, you are of immense importance to him.

In the meantime, if there is peril when prayer is too timid, the opposite doesn't represent a lesser danger, but an even greater one: to know if it is too overconfident. With respect to those who pray thus, with an excessive amount of assurance, listen to what the Lord said to the prophet: "Shout out, do not hold back! Lift up your voice like a trumpet!" (Isa 58:1). He said, "like a trumpet," for we must, with a vehement spirit, regain those who have experienced the trial of excessive confidence. "They seek me" (Isa 58:2), yet they haven't even found themselves!

Have you noticed that Bernard's tone here is harder and more severe? It is because the second danger which threatens prayer is almost more serious than the first: and we are even more responsible. Faithful, religious Christians must take a risk: the risk to find it normal that God hears them, to even estimate that God has a good chance to be able to count them amongst his few friends, or simply the risk to present themselves to God without astonishment, as if this comes from them, like as if it is taken for granted.

Faced with one of the things that he hates above all others, spiritual pride (the other is a lack of fervor), Bernard speaks here with the same authority as a prophet: his voice will be like a trumpet by which God himself said: "they seek me"— yes, they pray to me—"without even finding themselves"—in other words: without discerning to what point their assurance in themselves is ridiculous and undermines their prayers from the inside.

But if the first ones hear that, will they not sink more into their unhealthy timidness? Bernard explains:

> I don't say this to remove the confidence in prayer of the sinners, but I would like them to pray in the manner of a people who practiced sin, not righteousness (see Isa 58:2). May they pray for forgiveness of their sins with a "contrite heart and a humble spirit" (Dan 3:39), like the tax collector who said: "God be merciful to me, a sinner" (Lk 18:13).

No, it is not a question of falling back into a fear of God and paralyzing guilt which have nothing to do with holiness. We must enter into, and continuously renew ourselves in, this healthy and holy humility where the certainty of God's mercy is even greater than our consciousness of having the need for his grace, and where our assurance of God always remains astonished, when faced with his generosity, in order not to become— as if nothing matters—a sense of complacency in ourselves.

There is a third obstacle:

The third peril which threatens prayer is that it may be lukewarm instead of bursting forth from a vivid spark of our affective strengths.

We are surprised and confused: the spark of our affective strengths, in other words, the spark of our desire, that has become fervor, and here, the opposite of lukewarmness—is this not a theme that we have seen in the two previous chapters? Why did Bernard speak of this here only in passing? Patience: we will find it!

Let us simply read the summary that Bernard now gives of his teachings about prayer: first in a negative form, then in its positive form. He speaks of prayer—it's an image—like our embassy in heaven. And we note from it that by denouncing the three risks of prayer and bringing to light the three qualities that oppose them, he shows under what conditions God could receive and fulfill our prayers.

Thus, in this way, timid prayer does not reach heaven (see Sir 35:21), for a fearful expression compresses the spirit so much that prayer is unable, I will not say of arising, but simply of flowing. Lukewarm prayer arises only by dragging itself, then collapses through a lack of vigor. Prayer that is too assured lifts itself up, certainly, but falls back down; it encounters resistance, and not only does it not obtain grace, it draws a refusal.

To the contrary, if prayer is confident, humble, and fervent, it can be sure of reaching heaven and not "returning empty-handed" (Jer 50:9).

REFLECTION QUESTIONS

When I pray, do I pray with a feeling that I am not worthy to communicate with God? Am I too timid? Do I pray with too much self-assurance, that it is a given that God will give me what I want? Is my prayer full of demands, things that I see fit for myself? Does my prayer lack vigor? Or do I pray with a respect for God's mercy and his generosity, with the trust that he alone knows what I need from him?

The Fulfillment of Prayer

FOCUS POINT

The focus of our prayer should be God. Our desire in prayer—our goal in praying—is communion with God. Every part of our lives, our daily activities, the books we read, the thoughts we think, should be directed towards God. Why, then, should our prayer be any different? And our prayer will be fulfilled by God. This fulfillment might not be exactly—or anywhere near—what we envisioned, but there will be fulfillment. God is aware of what we need. And, through our praying, we are made more conscious of what our true needs are.

Nevertheless, each time that I speak about prayer, I seem to hear some very human thoughts come from your heart that I have often heard from others, having experienced them myself

31

at times in my own heart. In fact, how can we explain this: we never stop praying yet it seems that we practically never know, through experience, what the fruit of that prayer is? As much as we pray and continue to pray, no one ever responds with the least little word, no one gives us anything, it seems as if we have toiled in vain.[5]

⸻

The preceding chapter gave the conditions for a prayer that God could fulfill. Here, Saint Bernard starts from an even more distant notion: how to believe that God fulfills prayers? And we will see that this very direct question, at times, even bothers such a man of faith, as indicated in the opening chapter.

How can we respond to this disillusioning experience? It has the appearance of being real: its only fault is forgetting that the question of prayer should first be addressed to God, and not to ourselves—about God's promises, and not about our human experience, which is sensory and immediate. (But, in the next chapter, we will see that this is another kind of experience which does not oppose faith: to the contrary, it is used by faith.)

However, in the gospel, the Lord said: "Do not judge by appearances, but judge by right judgment" (Jn 7:24). But what is a right judgment if it is not a judgment of faith? For "the one who is righteous will live by faith" (Gal 3:11). So, trust in the judgment of faith and not in your own experience because faith is trustworthy and experience is not. And what is the truth of faith, if it is not the promise that the Son of God made to us himself: "whatever you ask for in prayer, believe that you have received it, and it will be yours" (Mk 11:24).

What do we perceive then, by placing ourselves thus at this level of faith and confidence in God's promises? We perceive something that astounds us: the cost, value, and the importance of our prayer to God.

> Brothers, no one amongst you should make little of prayer. For I tell you this: the One to whom we address our prayers is far from making little of it. "Even before a word is on my tongue" (Ps 139:4), you wrote them in your book (see Ps 139:16).

Now we can correctly ask the question about the fulfillment of prayer. Yes, with confidence, we must ask what we feel is good and necessary of God. But prayer isn't only a request on our part, it is also a progressive and patient discovery of that which God wants for us. Spontaneously, we begin from the idea that we must allow God entrance into our desire, and we will come to discover that it requires more, perhaps, to make our desire agree with the one that God has for us. From this I could no longer conclude that God has not fulfilled me; I will continue to pray in order to discover how he fulfills me.

> Here, then, is the uncontestable hope that we have: one of two things—he will give to us what we ask of him (see Jn 16:23), if he sees something useful for us in it. "For we do not know how to pray as we ought" (Rom 8:26), but he feels sorry for us and our ignorance and, by receiving our prayer with goodness, if something is absolutely useless, or not immediately

necessary to us, he will not give it to us. If our prayer
does just that, then it would not be unprofitable.

Why then would it not be unprofitable? Or rather, under what
conditions would it not be? Bernard readily replied:

> If we conform to the exhortation of the psalm, in other
> words, if we have put our delight in God. David, the
> Saint, in fact said: "Take delight in the Lord, and he
> will give you the desires of your heart" (Ps 37:4).

Take our "delight" in the Lord? Yes, so that our prayer will
truly become the agreement of our desire with that of God, we
must first have this conviction: God, more lucidly than I, and
even better than I, knows and wants my true well-being.

What is my true well-being? That is a way of speaking that
is a bit abstract and theoretical. My "delights" are much more
concrete! Yes, this great need and taste for pleasure within me,
this aspiration of a plenitude of existence which orders my
affective life, and the spark of desire: that is what we must
bring together and put into God, invest in God—in other words,
conversion.

Here we see the heart of our theme: the conversion of desire. We also see a connection with the end of the last chapter,
which has perhaps left us wanting more: the mobilization of
the affective forces so that they become the fervor of a prayer
that God could then fulfill. And we then make an essential
discovery: if God is my delight, my prayer could then ask all
sorts of things of him, it would always be him that it desires.
This conversion throws new light upon the question of fulfillment of prayer and its essential procedure.

We must not just pay God "lip service" in prayer. So that

God is my delight, the Psalmist doesn't speak about an experience that is reserved for a few privileged mystical persons, but as a condition in which God grants me "the desires of my heart." However, our feelings of pleasure are on the sensory level, and are connected to the realities here and now. Perhaps we have had the experience that God and his requirements for holiness are the opposite of what we consider to be pleasure. How can we pretend that pleasure, which is effectively and inevitably a factor of experience, could have God as its aim and objective? Saint Bernard will explain this to us in the next chapter.

REFLECTION QUESTIONS

In what state of mind do I enter prayer? Am I aware of the fact that the goal of my prayer time is God, a closer union with God? Am I open to the promptings and guidance of God during my prayer? Or am I too focused on asking for those things that *I* think I need? Do I delight in the presence of God during prayer? Is prayer a restful and refreshing time for me? If I find prayer to be a constant labor, how can I change my outlook and approach to allow for God's wonder and the refreshing communication of prayer to enter into my life?

DAY SIX

Prayer:
The Conversion of Desire

FOCUS POINT

Prayer is a unifying experience. It combines understanding and desire, reason and affectivity. Prayer is not simply feeling; nor is prayer merely reduced to the intellect. True prayer is unifying; that is, it incorporates the entire person, bringing him or her entirely to God. Our desire to understand God should be of the utmost importance in prayer. Desire. Understanding. Faith seeking understanding, in our lives, in our prayer-lives. God wants us entirely present to him in prayer. God wants every part of our person open to him in prayer.

Yet, O prophet, why is your tone so absolute, as you exhort us to find our delight in the Lord, as if this was within our reach? Yes, we know the delights of food, sleep, rest, and all that one could find on earth. But God, what does he present to us in terms of delight so that we could find our delight in him?[6]

This passage from Bernard's *Sermons for Lent* reminds us of the Scripture quotation that Bernard commented on in the last chapter (which he will continue to explain to us in this chapter): "Take delight in the Lord, and he will give you the desires of your heart" (Ps 37:4).

In Day 5, we had stopped our discussion at the question of how to know that this granting of our heart's desires could be realized for us in truth, and even how, if such an experience, which the Psalmist however considered necessary for us, is possible. And, in fact, Bernard went beyond simple words. On our behalf, he questioned the Psalmist (whom he called "Prophet"), and here is the answer that Bernard records:

Who, amongst you, has not experienced the inherent delight of a good conscience, experienced the desire and the taste for chastity, humility, and charity? These delights are surely not the same as those which come from food or drink or other manner of similar things; they are, nonetheless, delights, and much greater than all those that we have just listed. These delights are divine, not sensual. It is in the Lord that we will find these delights of chastity, humility, and charity.

What Bernard is aiming at here is to show us how to go beyond the first experiences of earthly, bodily pleasures to another experience which is spiritual.

Have we not ever lived the gospel, not only in an interior battle, but in peace within ourselves, and in agreement with a profound conviction? (That is what a "good conscience" here means—an expression borrowed from the pastoral epistles.) Has it ever happened that we discern, in chastity, marriage, or celibacy, not only a virtue that takes all of our strength, but a true and happy reality of our love? Has it ever happened that we experience humility no longer as a type of death but, at times, like an attitude that spontaneously and profoundly expresses who we are? To manifest love not only as an expensive renouncement, but as a means by which our heart experiences happiness?

Yes? But then, Bernard said, where does this interior agreement (which is a good conscience, consisting of the graces of chastity, humility, and charity) come from? From God, certainly. So, beyond that, you discover that it is by the spiritual experience of putting these delights in God that you find your pleasure in him.

But then—oh horror—there is a considerable objection, even a double objection, which seems to dash not only what Bernard is developing, but the very phrase of the Psalmist:

But perhaps there may be many who will object that this interior sensory spark, a delight, and sweeter than honey and the drippings of the honeycomb (Ps 119:10), is experienced so rarely. In fact, by reason of the temptations they face in this life, they behave more strongly by practicing these same virtues, not with the goal of a delight that they experience, but in view of these virtues themselves. And this is for the sole goal of pleasing God, with complete determination, even if it isn't with their whole feelings.

There is a double objection: first, this spiritual experience of delight in God, where all of my subjectivity agrees with what God expects from me, is far from being normal. Can I then count on it to pray and serve God? In other respects: is it not only more sure, but more generous, for me to do everything to please God, rather than asking myself if it pleases me?

We are astonished to hear Bernard tell us: that is exactly along the same lines as what the Psalmist said!

> Nevertheless, let us not have doubts: such an attitude better fulfills the Prophet's invitation when he said, "Take delight in the Lord"; for he did not speak of sensory desires here, but of a style of life to put into practice. Such a desire aims at happiness, this putting into practice has virtue as its goal.

Truly, doesn't Bernard seem to be contradictory? Unless his train of thought, in this paragraph, is simply not developed enough. Isn't the key to understanding it in the last phrase: in the verb "aim" and the term "goal"? It is as if Bernard said: by itself, affectivity aims at an egocentric happiness, evidently that is not what we're speaking about here. To aim at my happiness is to certainly miss God. It is God we must aim for, and thus "virtue" (the terms means strength); to put into practice a new style of life, without renouncing to find in it, as a bonus, our happiness. But the "goal" is not to find it there, but to "put" it there—the emphasis in the psalmist's phrase relies on this imperative.

That is precisely the conversion of desire and all affective strengths: to renounce making them as the goal of a spiritual life or criteria for the quality of prayer, but to resolutely engage them in the movement of prayer, which is nothing other than the movement of faith. To not wait, by enchantment, for our delights to be spontaneously found in the Lord, but to take them in him, thrust them at him. For fervor, which is indispensable, is nothing more than this.

All of this is explained in the following passage:

> "Take delight in the Lord," he said: yes, gather and direct your strengths and your efforts in a way so that you can take delight in the Lord, "and he will give you the desire of your heart" (Ps 37:4).

We readily find concordance between understanding and affectivity in the following:

> But be careful: by speaking about the desire of your heart, he hears those which are approved by judgment of reason.

Thus, prayer is presented as a privileged moment where the spark of desire—the heart—is called to unite with the judgment of reason, which, as we know, is the instance in us when we receive the light of faith.

Let us keep the end of the passage for the next chapter.

REFLECTION QUESTIONS
When I pray, am I aware of being totally present to God? Is my prayer time one of faith seeking understanding? Do I have a desire to know God better through my praying? Or is my prayer time simply a wish list of my desires? Or are my prayers simply a recitation of memorized passages lacking a desire to know God? In what ways can I be more present to God in my praying? How can I become a better listener in my prayer life?

Gratitude: Grace and Thanksgiving

FOCUS POINT

Much of our life—including our prayer life—should be spent in giving thanks to God for all he has given and all he continues to give us. This gratitude can well up and spring forth from our hearts, if there is a place in our hearts for thanksgiving to reside. Humility is the key. If we can be humble people, not allowing ourselves to be filled with pride and illusion, we will have a place where gratitude can flourish and we can give thanks to God in our prayer.

You have no reason to complain; to the contrary, how can you not put all of the spark of your desire into thanksgiving, seeing with how much great care God surrounds you? In fact, each time, through ignorance, you ask for something that is useless to you; instead of listening to you, he grants you a more useful gift instead.7

If we think now about all that motivated Bernard's teachings about prayer as the conversion of desire, we will remember that it is comprised of knowing what prayers God could fulfill. In this regard, Bernard, in Sermon V of *Sermons for the Season of Lent*, continues his discussion of the last chapter in the above passage.

What does this passage mean, if not that the role of subjectivity, converted through fervor, appears to be particularly like that of thanksgiving? Not only the gratitude that follows fulfillment, once it is recognized, but an act of thanksgiving that precedes it. Precedes it, yes, so much so that I will know that the prayer is not an effort to oblige God to fulfill me, but an act of confidence which seeks to discern how my request will unite with the fulfillment that God prepared for it. And how my desire will coincide with the desire that God has for me—and of me.

Gratitude and praise—a totally new way to see everything, oneself, and others. Is that not God's way?

But if the spark of desire, which became fervor by turning itself towards God, expresses gratitude, it is necessary to note that, in return, gratitude is indispensable to keep fervor and spiritual willingness alive.

By thinking of the method to conversion by which Christ's disciple wants to let the grace of God fill him completely, Bernard outlines the steps of this method, which involves humility. Humility? Yes, what space is left for grace, when the person is full of himself? It is then that we must break with the sins to which we have become accustomed, and confess them, so that God may forgive, and by changing our lifestyle in order to open ourselves to grace. (That is what Bernard calls, as in Scripture, "Carrying the fruit of repentance.") But to be able to do it properly, easily, as if it was unknown to us, could turn us away from humility, centering us upon ourselves, be it through a bad conscience (where our sin clouds us as if it is stronger than God's mercy) or through too good a conscience (where our virtues marvel us as if they came from us).

Then, Saint Bernard shouts:

> But you will be unhappy if ingratitude succeeds them, it is perhaps more injurious than vice and sin. In all evidence, what could be more opposed to grace? With time, the fervor of our conversion will dwindle, charity will grow cold (Mt 24:12), little by little, iniquity will increase so much and so well that we will end with the flesh that which we started in the Spirit (Gal 3:3). The consequence will be that we will not know how to recognize the gifts that God has given us (see 1 Cor 2:12); will we be closed as much to spiritual willingness as to gratitude? (...)
>
> If we show ourselves available to God, attentive and ardent in spirit (Rom 12:11), we must take care not to place our trust in our own merits or rest on our own laurels. Otherwise, grace cannot enter into this soul. Evidently, it is already full and there's no space left in it for grace.[8]

We say the words "say thank you" to a child so often that it almost seems instinctual for us to take rather than receive and the spontaneous desire to possess without owing anything to anyone. Yes, for many it is difficult to give, and it is even more difficult to receive.

Inversely, if we harshly resent having offered something or proposing a service to someone without receiving gratitude for it, in this way, this gift or service misses its mark. It sort of remains in our hands, in our heart; we almost regret having offered it. This feeling of failure that comes from this gift or service means much more than it really is: it expresses the essential reciprocity between people, it symbolizes communion.

However, in the world of humans relations, that is an echo of a law which characterizes grace completely. This is not something, but an act or gesture by God, of which I lose the effect, and which I even render impossible, if I detach it from God. We could say the same thing in another way: by closing my hand around a gift from God, by considering it as belonging to me in a possessive attitude, I become unable to receive it.

The words are full of meaning: "give" thanks, "gratitude." To give thanks to God, and bring it to him, by recognizing that it is from him, allows us to give and give again to him endlessly. And that is how the conversion of desire, within us, is truly fulfilled through thanksgiving, since, if in its first spark, it is turned to ourselves, it is only our desire to get something and our refusal to owe anything to anyone.

Bernard—after many different passages of Scripture—by looking at water flowing, liked to recognize a symbol in nature for this law of grace:

> However, it is not because Christ needs it that he asks again for what he had given, but it is to keep to your advantage all that you would decide to give him. Ef-

fectively, if the water of a river stagnates, it will spoil and, by overflowing, it pushes back the water that is still flowing to it. It is the same for grace: it stops flowing unless we bring it back to its source; and for a man without gratitude, it ceases, not only to increase, but what he had previously received turns against him. To the contrary, the one who shows himself faithful for the little that is entrusted to him, will be judged worthy of a greater consequent gift (see Lk 19:17).[9]

REFLECTION QUESTIONS

How do I nurture humility in my life? How do I clear a space in my heart and in my mind so that the pride and distraction that so often fill me will not keep me from my goal (God, praising God)? How much of my prayer life involves praising God for who he is and what he gives, and how much of it involves asking God for what I want? What are some new and different ways I can praise God and show gratitude to him?

DAY EIGHT

Seeking God .

FOCUS POINT

God is the source of everything in our lives. We cannot even
approach God in prayer without God giving us the grace to do
so. Our desire to seek God comes from God. Knowledge precedes desire. To know God is love him, and we know God
because he is with us, always, as he promised in chapter 28,
verse 20 of the Gospel of Matthew. God is a part of all of us,
he is with us, and he calls us to seek him, providing us always
with the grace to do so.

*What will I say to those who seek him or those who possess
him? For those who have him and, at the same time, seek him;
for, unless they possess him, they cannot seek him. (...) Engen-
dered by the Word-made-flesh, they possess the Word-made-*

*flesh. However, is not the Word-made-flesh the Lord? Listen
to what John said: "and the Word was God." What more does
the generation of those who possess the Lord seek? (...)*

*And, truth be told, without seeking him, they could pos-
sess him, but without possessing him, it is impossible to seek
him. It is about itself that Wisdom speaks in these terms: "For
those who eat of me will hunger for more" (Sir 24:21). He is
so powerful that he offers himself to those who do not seek
him, since—we have already shown—from the time of the fulfillment of his grace, and his blessing, which is full of tender-
ness, he seeks and predisposes those who are not yet able to
seek him. But no one, before possessing him, is able to seek
him, as he, himself, said: "No one can come to me unless drawn
by the Father" (Jn 6:44). Therefore, he is present, the One
who draws us to him, but, in a certain way, he is not yet present,
since he draws to no one but himself. In fact, the Father is
never present through faith without the Son being there, in
order to draw everyone to come see him*[10] *(Sermon on the
Psalm "Who Lives," Sermon XVII).*

B efore beginning the meditation for today, let us remember
two points that were made in the last chapter: though whatever is asked from God, it is he that is desired in the end; and
thanksgiving constitutes our concrete way of not separating
grace from God who gives it to us.

The opening passage from *Sermon on the Psalm "Who
Lives"* places squarely before us what is essential for our existence here on earth: seeking God. Bernard asked the questions
in this passage after the following experience: One summer
day, at harvest time, Saint Bernard was returning from a trip.

Seeing his abbey from afar, and thinking about those who were gathered there, these following words imposed themselves on his spirit: "Such is the company of those who seek him" (Ps 24:6). (For monastic life promises nothing more than organizing people together in the most radical way in view of this search for God.)

To seek in order to find: that is what life on earth is, for the most part. And happily, we may find what we are seeking. The paradox with God is that, by seeking him, we realize that we have found him (if we could call it that). But he is the one who finds and unites us in Jesus first.

To seek because we have found: that is a perfect contradiction, humanly speaking. But it is an incredible truth (however believable), when God is concerned. The Fathers of the Church liked to say it: Saint Augustine, Saint Gregory the Great.... And in the same way, Bernard says it here in a magnificent way.

For me to feel such radical desire—a desire that is always ready to invest itself in no matter what, but then a desire that is soon disappointed—for me to profoundly feel such an immense desire, a desire for everything, could I not have an inkling that this desire is within me, like an indication, a hidden sign, indicating the One who created me?

And if my desire now, which is spontaneously all encompassing, and egocentric as well, encounters Christ, and if I allow myself to be regenerated through his Word, in faith and baptism, what will become of this desire that I am? It will become a search for this Lord who sought me, through whom I allowed myself to be found, and in whom I recognize God, the source of this desire, and the only one who can fulfill it one day.

Because, for the moment, I do not meet God directly, I do

not see him with my own eyes, I do not have an immediate experience of him. And I could conclude that he is not there, absent from the world, and my life. No. It is a time for faith and hope, the time for a meeting, but an indirect one, the time for a mediating experience. I seek God and, by doing this, I have the experience that he is present for me in this very search. For to come to God is, forcibly, to experience the attraction which is Christ. In the absence of meeting him before me, objectively, I discover him behind me, subjectively. He is present in the movement of my search and the attraction that I feel; present in the conversion of my desire.

Isn't it marvelous? Yes.

Isn't it terrible? Yes.

Terrible in terms of a spiritual requirement, when I know how much the desire within me remains plural, changing, intermittent, distracted by the least thought, seized by the least sensation, by fleeing from what is difficult. Is it then necessary that prayer incessantly reshapes itself to this desire, that it asks God to give me a hunger for him, that it lives the Eucharist as if it is an occasion to deepen this hunger, that it begs Christ to draw me to follow him? That is exactly Bernard's conclusion:

> This race, in fact, is not within the realm of human possibility, it is the right hand of the Lord that unfolds its strength (see Ps 118:16), you must also constantly cry out to him: "your name is perfume poured out...draw me after you" (Song 1:3, 4).

Isn't this also marvelous? Yes, in so much as it has terrible requirements, this search for God is full of joy, gladness, and the proof of his presence:

How then can my spirit now not rejoice in God (Lk 1:47)? How can I not be transported by infinite gladness, amongst the generation of those who seek the Lord? For to feel such a violent hunger for him is a very credible witness of a wisdom that has already been abundantly experienced. Yes, for me it is absolute and certain proof and an indisputable indicator: you possess him, since you seek him in this way, and he dwells in you, since he draws you to him with such force.

REFLECTION QUESTIONS

Am I aware of God's dwelling within me, giving me the grace to call upon him and seek him out? In my prayer, do I call on God to increase my desire for and my understanding of him? Do I feel the love of God in my life? How do I feel when I realize that God initiates everything in my relationship with him? Do I feel that love? Do I feel that special love God has for me when I realize that even my ability to love God comes from God through his grace?

Our Holiness Is a Work in Progress

FOCUS POINT

There is a significant space that concerns us all: the space between the people we are and the people we are called to be. This space can be quite discouraging. But God's mercy must always be kept in mind. God's mercy is infinite, it knows no bounds. Keeping this in mind, we come to realize that the road to holiness, the road to perfecting ourselves, is a road we cannot expect to walk alone. God's grace and mercy are a must, and they are with us always. Therefore, any stumbling or any sin along the way should not discourage us for very long, as long we remember to get up and remain steadfast in our faith— God is with us every step of the way.

Yes, we seem and are poor; but if we have received "the Spirit that is from God, so that we may understand the gifts bestowed on us from God" (1 Cor 2:12), the glory is great, the power that is given to us by him is also great. "But to all who received him...he gave power to become children of God" (Jn 1:12). Do we not possess this power of the children of God when absolutely everything is at our service? In fact, the Apostle knew: "all things work together for good for those who love God" (Rom 8:28)[11] (Sermons for Sundays in November, Sermon 1).

I n this passge from *Sermons for Sundays in November,* Bernard discusses a famous teaching from Saint Paul. These clear and enlightening words seem to contradict the idea we had at the end of the previous chapter—that when we think about all that the conversion of our desire requires, that it is a terrible requirement. Saint Bernard didn't deny this—he exhorted us to this conversion throughout his *Sermons for the Seasons of the Church.* The problem, then, is this: how can we make arrangements so that we do not falter under the weight of this requirement; how can we not lose our courage; how can we not turn the Christian life into an unfortunate constraint; and, finally, how could we not hate either the requirement (and God at the same time) or ourselves?

Bernard foresaw this objection—even more than that, this refusal to accept this:

But one of you could perhaps say, "What does it matter to me?" while rehashing in your cowardly heart such thoughts: "Yes, may they glorify themselves in their power as children of God, those whose filial love for God burns within themselves, those in whom the spark of desire is full of vigor; and may they then anticipate that everything will be for their own good, those who love God in truth" (see 1 Jn 3:18). "But I am poor and needy" (Ps 40:17), lacking in filial spark, and a spiritual willingness that is worthy of God.

It is then the spark of desire that is in question, as well as the fervor, of which it should be the fuel. This passage from Saint Paul might not concern me, but it may condemn me, declares the one who calls himself poor and needy here, but in a negative way. No, it doesn't concern me because I don't love God: I don't experience an ardor, I do not feel a willingness, I do not live a search that would be worthy of him.

Who is speaking here, if it is not someone who is lukewarm in their faith? And when we know that, along with pride, lukewarmness is what Bernard hates the most, we can imagine the storm of words that is going to follow....

A storm of words? No. And not even a commiseration, but firm and serene words, which are filled with a sense of equilibrium:

> Be very attentive to what follows: he leaves no motive of despair in his writings, he who said, in another passage: "For whatever was written in former days was written for our instruction, so that by steadfastness and by encouragement of the scriptures we might have hope" (Rom 15:4).
>
> This spark of love that you claim to have is peace, not patience; however we will find peace in the homeland, not on the path that takes one there, and those

who have this peace will not have the need to be consoled by the Scriptures.

Let us turn our attention to this term "peace," which we must
understand here in its most absolute sense: peace as an absence of interior conflict, like a perfect equilibrium within ourselves, like a spiritual stability in the face of all trials. In other
words, the "homeland" is the kingdom of God. You are dream-
ing that you have made it, Bernard explains, and thus you
refuse, you deny reality. We are on the path throughout our
entire Christian life, and walking along it is to find an equilibrium again which never ceases being put into question.

To how many Christians could he not say this today? To
you, perhaps? To how many Christians who can't tolerate the
distance between the perfection they aim for (and dream about),
and the part of it which they achieve for this moment; to those
who live this distance as a failure, a hypocrisy, and a constant
reproach. They feel that it is an unfathomable chasm, instead
of awaiting a call, which is the "hope" that the Apostle invites
us to renew by reading the Scriptures—the hope that brings
both the "patience" and perseverance to strive towards the
goal, and "consolation" at not yet having reached it yet.

Bernard then reminds us of the terms to deploy the strength
of our conviction:

Whether through patience, then, or by the conviction
of the Scriptures, we may have hope, even if we have
not yet acquired peace. That is why, after having said
that all will come to good for those who love God, the
Apostle explained, "those who are called (saints) according to his purpose" (Rom 8:28). The term "saints"
in this phrase should not worry you, since it is not due

to merit, but it is with reference to a project that they are called saints, but not by reason of the feelings they have experienced, but due to the goal pursued.

In this passage, it is the term "project" that draws our attention. Bernard cites a version of Romans 8:28 that is no longer ours. It goes marvelously in the sense of what he wants to demonstrate: your holiness, your desire for God, and your fervor are a work in progress. You do not have to appreciate them according to what you subjectively or affectively feel—that would be turning it towards you. Understand project to mean the goal of your faith. And if your feelings and the spark of your desire appear to be unworthy of God, you only have one solution: put them more vigorously into this vision, redirect them towards the goal, patiently convert them. May your affective strengths reach to unite with your faith.

It is in this sense that the Prophet affirmed: "Preserve my life, for I am holy" (see Ps 86:2). Paul, so weighed down by the heaviness of his corruptible flesh, did not himself believe that he had attained this holiness. He simply said: "...forgetting what lies behind and straining forward to what lies ahead, I press on toward the goal for the prize of the heavenly call of God in Jesus Christ" (Phil 3:13–14). Thus, you see that, without having yet won the prize, he continues to press toward the goal for the prize of holiness.

Thus, you also, if you resolve to depart from evil and do good (Ps 37:27) in your heart, to persevere in what you have undertaken, and to ceaselessly make progress towards it, and if—in as much as, at times, you act with less righteousness through human weakness—you decide to not persist in this stumbling, but to repent and mend your ways as much as you can, then, yes, without a doubt, you will be holy and you will also find the need, at that time, to shout: "Preserve my life, for I am holy."

In order to convince us, Bernard cited this verse from psalm 86 at both the beginning and the end of this passage. Between the two, he gave the explanation. The words of the Psalmist prove themselves to be paradoxical: if its holiness is a definitive perfection of the soul, why ask God for it to be preserved?

Bernard explains, with an admirable pertinence, that for Paul, at that time, holiness is not to find himself at the goal, but on the road to it, and that it consists of not returning to his previous feelings and staying with them, but to thrust his whole being forward in the race to holiness.

Finally, reread the last paragraph: it is marvelous. A single phrase, long and sinuous like life itself! And it tells you that, in the project of faith and hope, stumblings are not failures (as long as they don't deter you) but opportunities to call upon the strength of forgiveness to put you back on the path more ardently.

Are we not witnessing directly all of the dynamism of a conception of Christian life whose requirement is not moral, but "mystical"?

REFLECTION QUESTIONS

Am I easily discouraged in my spiritual life? Do I keep in mind God's mercy, generosity, and grace during those periods when I feel less than holy, when I have stumbled in my faith? Am I able to forgive myself when I stumble in my journey, knowing that it is human to sin? Am I able to get to my feet after such a fall, and remain faithful to focusing on my ultimate goal, union with God in heaven?

DAY TEN

With God During Suffering

FOCUS POINT

Suffering is a part of all of our lives. There is a grace God gives to us all in the midst of our suffering, and that is knowing his presence throughout our trials. God suffered as well, and during our own suffering we can unite our pain to his, and experience unity with God in this area of our lives—an area that might otherwise seem devoid of all meaning. But there is meaning in suffering, the prelude to death. God conquered suffering and death, gracing the penalty of Adam's sin with God's holy presence. Suffering is sanctified, and we share in God's suffering through our own trials.

*"We boast in our hope of sharing the glory of God" (Rom
5:2), "while we wait for the blessed hope and the manifesta-
tion of the glory of our great God and Savior, Jesus Christ"
(Titus 2:13). But there is more. And to express it better, let us
glorify ourselves in suffering, for it is through suffering that
the hope for glory is found (see Rom 5:3ff). See if this isn't the
same thing as the Apostle wanted to teach about when he added:
"suffering produces endurance..." (Rom 5:3)12 (Sermon on
the Psalm "Who Lives," Sermon XVII).*

———

Saint Bernard comments here on God's promise in psalm
91:15: "I will be with them in trouble." He begins by af-
firming: "suffering is a necessity."

This is not a statement that is well-received nowadays. We
don't like such ideas, we suspect—not always wrongly so—
that they express a morbid taste for suffering, or at least a
passive manner of allowing oneself to be beaten down by them
and a too easy justification for unhappiness.

You may not want to subscribe to this theory of "necessity," that is fine. But for you, personally, are you really sure
that such an affirmation is coming from another era? First:
doesn't suffering make up an inevitable part of human life?
What meaning, then, can we give to it? Can you imagine following Christ without having to carry his cross, living the beatitudes without being among those who cry in order to be
consoled, or welcoming the gospel without violently throwing
yourself against that which opposes it, both in yourself and in
the world around you?

Yes, suffering is a necessity. It is a consequence of faith and
obedience, and even a way to choose to love God and our

neighbor. Bernard affirms this necessity without feeling the need to justify it. He knows himself to be part of a tradition that goes back all the way to Jesus and the apostles.

He explains that if suffering is a necessity, it is because it takes on a positive meaning. It reveals itself to be

> useful because it is a test, and carries one to glory. Sadness is also a necessity, one that changes into joy, and need (lack, indigence) is also necessary: it gives birth to the crown.

Can it be said that we purchase future salvation with suffering? Oh no, salvation cannot be purchased; it is received…through suffering. Here, Bernard takes Saint Paul seriously and holds him to the letter of his word in what he has that is paradoxical: to glorify ourselves in suffering.

That is what the Apostle effectively affirmed: what is realized in the initial verses of Romans 5. This future of glory, that is hope, is already found to be present in suffering (just as the fruit is already present in the seed). Suffering itself is an experience of glory. Remember that from the time suffering appears to you, it is a way of choosing the future in God. Make suffering the goal of your life.

> In fact, it is through suffering that the hope for glory is found. Moreover, it is in suffering that glory itself is found, just like the hope for the fruit is found in the seed, and, thus, the fruit itself is in the seed.
>
> From now on, the kingdom of God is among you (Lk 17:21), this (immense) treasure in clay jars (2 Cor 4:7), hidden in a field (Mt 13:44). It is here, yes, but hidden. Happy are those who would have found it.

Who will they be?—Those who would have manifested more attention to the harvest than to the seeding.

For the moment, let us hurry to buy this field in order to acquire the treasure that can be found hidden there. Let us consider it nothing but joy (Jas 1:2) to fall into all sorts of suffering.

Are you surprised to find such a willingness to welcome suffering in Bernard, and, at the same time, a tone that is so free and so masochistic? You are correct to feel surprised—the better to admire this mystery. Bernard comes back now to the verse of the psalm, after this detour that deploys all its strength:

> God said: "I will be with them in trouble" (Ps 91:15). In the meantime, will I seek something other than suffering? (...)
>
> He is with us with a bounty of grace: in the bounty of glory, we will be with him. He will descend (1 Thess 4:16) to rescue us (Ps 34:19), to be with us in our suffering. "We will be caught up in the clouds together with them to meet the Lord in the air; and so we will be with the Lord forever" (1 Thess 4:17)—as long as we would have taken care, in the meantime, to have always been with him, so that he will accompany us on our path, and the One who should give us our homeland. Even more, so that he will be the way (Jn 14:6), he will be the homeland.
>
> It is better for me, Lord, to have suffering, as long as you are with me, rather than ruling, feasting, or knowing glory without you. It is better even for me to keep you in my embrace through suffering, and passing through the furnace with you, than to be without you,

even in heaven. "Whom have I in heaven but you? And there is nothing on earth that I desire other than you" (Ps 73:25).

It is not that suffering, in itself, is useful, necessary, and, in fact, desirable. No, it is because of the promise: the Lord is with us in it. But it is also because we would have "taken care to have always been with him." In other words, suffering will be our way to choose him, to give ourselves to him, to belong to him and trust him, and, in all of this, to mysteriously enjoy his presence.

The "necessity" for suffering—one does not have to affirm it as if it is a general abstract principle, but as if it is the fruit of a personal experience, to bring up and acknowledge in prayer:

> *Yes, Lord Jesus, gold must be purified and its quality attested to by fire. In the same way, it is impossible for the spark of my desire to turn itself entirely towards you, and unite itself with your fatherly love, without dying and being reborn through the trials of suffering. But, O marvel, when suffering is accepted, it is not only a trial, but a privileged moment between us where I unite myself with you, and where I find you by choosing you. Then I will be able to say, with your servant Bernard...*

Why tremble or hesitate, why flee from this furnace? The fire breaks out, yes, but the Lord is with us in suffering. If "God is for us, who is against us?" (Rom

8:31). In the same way, it is he who delivers us, who saves us from it with his hands; yes, who could snatch us out of his hands (see Jn 10:28)? Finally, it is he who glorifies, who else could deprive us of his glory? If it is he who glorifies, who humbles us?

REFLECTION QUESTIONS

When I suffer, am I aware of the presence of God in the midst of my trials? Do I feel a sense of peace knowing that suffering has been made holy by Jesus Christ? Knowing that suffering causes selfishness (in that it forces me to focus on myself so much), am I able to keep the suffering of others in mind and extend myself in prayer on their behalf during times of my own suffering?

Contemplate Christ: Humbled, Glorified

FOCUS POINT

Glory and humility. These words seem to be polar opposites. In fact, they are counterparts. How did Jesus appear to us? Humble, in the form of a servant. And he is God. Is there anyone more glorified in the universe than God? Our worldly definitions of glory may not include humility. But our worldly glories are prideful illusions, vacant of any true glory. Glory, in truth, has a foundation of humility, as evidenced by our God.

"I saw the Lord sitting on a throne, high and lofty;...the whole earth is full of his glory" (Isa 6:1, 3). It is a very high vision

that is described for us in this passage by the Prophet. He said,
"I saw the Lord sitting." The sight was a great one: blessed
are the eyes that see what you see (Lk 10:23). Who doesn't put
all of his desire and all of his covetousness into contemplating
the splendor of a similar glory? Yes, that was the desire of all
of the saints, all of the time. For it was the One at whom the
angels longed to look (1 Pet 1:12), and this is eternal life that
you see (see Jn 17:3).

But brothers, I hear the same Prophet speak, with regard
to the Lord, about another vision, which is extremely differ-
ent. Yes, Isaiah, in another passage, explained it thus: "he had
no form or majesty...he was despised and rejected by others..."
*(Isa 53:2, 3).*13

The theme of this chapter connects the theme of the last
one (the Lord with us during suffering) with the one which
builds upon our starting point: the Lord's humility.

The glory of God is not only worthy of our desire, but it
definitively surpasses it: it could never run out. Nevertheless,
the compulsory passage of desire, lest we escape from reality,
is Jesus who has come amongst us. In as much as the contem-
plative gaze, which is a loving one, does not make us specta-
tors, even less voyeurs. It only reveals itself to be authentic in
only as much as it transforms us to the image of the One we
love.

If you also want to see him in his elevation, first you
must be sure to see Jesus in his abasement. If you want
to see the King on his throne, start by looking at the
serpent in the wilderness (Jn 3:14). And may this first

vision humble you so that, humbled, you will be lifted up by the second. Yes, may that one humble you again and heal your arrogance, so that vision will fill you and fulfill your desire.

Do you see him humbled? (Phil 2:8). May this glimpse you have of him not be useless, for, at the same time, you could never uselessly see him exalted. You will be like him when he is revealed, for we will see him as he is (1 Jn 3:2); therefore, be like him now by seeing how he has become because of you. In fact, if, even in his abasement, you do not refuse to be like him, you can be assured, as if it is a given, to become like him in his elevation. He will never accept to see the one who had been associated with his suffering be kept away from the communion and his glory. He hesitates so little to receive, into his kingdom, the one who associates himself with his passion, that the criminal, after having confessed on the cross, will have been received into paradise with him on the same day (Lk 23:42, 43).

Why is this passage through the Lord's humility compulsory? Bernard said: our desire must be healed of its arrogance in order to be able to allow itself to be fulfilled. Yes, spontaneously we have a certain idea of the grandeur and the glory, which fills us of ourselves. Pride is not only a sin, it's an error, the choice of an "unreality." The conversion of desire does not start this surprising discovery. Humility and glory are not in a relationship of opposition, but one of reciprocity. The Son of God, when he abased himself all the way to live our life and die our death, is no less God—he was never more. His glory is his love. In the same way, the more that humility is a deliberate choice for us, a freedom in view of love, the more we approach our authentic grandeur and our truth.

It is here that prayer plays an indispensable role: in it, we are invited to unify, on the one hand, the Jesus of the gospel, the Jesus of the beatitudes and the passion, in a single regard, with, on the other hand, the concrete reality of our lives. In the latter case, what are the circumstances under which my desire for grandeur tends to harden me, to puff me up? And what are the occasions when I feel humbled by someone else, or by my limitations? How, then, can turning my attention to Christ become the way by which it brings me to discern between true and false grandeur? This is so I can know how to concretely choose to act, not through pride, but through generosity and forbearance (that is, the grandeur of the soul). And so that I reach this extreme freedom of the soul so I am able to transform a humiliation which unhinges me into royal humility.

What is the secret of such generosity and freedom? It rests much less in a moral constraint to exact on one's self than in a mystical love, always more fervent, for Christ. The next passage of Bernard's text says it magnificently:

> If we suffer with him, we will reign with him: as a result, my brothers, in this manner, all of our meditations are summed up in Christ, the crucified Christ (1 Cor 2:2). Let us place them like a seal on our hearts, like a seal upon our arm (Song 8:6). Let us open ourselves to him, in other words, give love that responds to his love, and let us follow him by the humble and attentive willingness of our manner of life.
>
> Such is the path at the end of which he will show himself to us in his own reality, he, himself, the salvation

of God (Ps 50:23); it will not then be without brilliance nor beauty, but he will appear in a splendor that
is so great that his glory will fill the whole earth (Ps
72:19).

REFLECTION QUESTIONS

In what ways do I attempt to be more humble? Am I aware of
the open space within me—created for God—when I am filled
with humility? If I am only aware of the worldly glories of
pride and selfishness within myself, how might prayer clear
out these false glories to make room for the peace of God that
accompanies humility? Are there any particular saints whose
lives speak to me as a special example of humility upon which
I might reflect and gain inspiration?

DAY TWELVE

A Dynamic Stability

FOCUS POINT

God is infinite. Even when we meet God in heaven, we will forever desire him. We will never tire of his love, goodness, mercy, and generosity. We will never fully know his love, goodness, mercy, and generosity, and because of this we will desire him all the more throughout eternity. We seek to know God here on earth, amongst the instability of our daily lives. This seeking will not end at death, it will never rest because there will always be more of God to be experienced. God is immeasurable.

In my opinion, even if we have found him once, we will never stop seeking him. (...) The happiness in finding him will not satisfy a holy desire, to the contrary, it amplifies it. By attaining the bounty, will the joy consume the desire? No, it adds more oil to the one who is the flame. Yes, it is truly like this: gladness will reach its bounty, but the desire will never end, and, consequently, neither will the search. But try to imagine, if you can, a search that never ends when we want for nothing, and a desire that is not accompanied with worry![14] *(Sermons on the Canticle of Canticles, Sermon LXXXIV).*

B y reflecting upon holiness, we should have recognized, with Saint Bernard, that it doesn't consist solely of a stability, a permanence, but in the dynamism of a progression, an incessant conversion. Is it, then, in the eternal kingdom that we will know stability? Certainly. But will the absence of all movement and everything new delight us very much? So many people today fear being mortally bored for all eternity….

In Bernard's era, they knew less fear, because change did not appear to be of as much value as in our time. Nevertheless, desire, in Bernard's eyes, also essentially defines the human being, so that we might imagine that desire might disappear when our resurrection comes. But, will the happiness of eternity put an end to the dynamic which is so fundamental to love: to seek God in order to better find him, to find him in order to better seek him, to know him to better desire him?

Truly, this is unimaginable here on earth. Yet we can understand it, what a happy way to evoke eternity; and what a beautiful and just image is the bounty of joy, that comes flowing upon desire like oil on a fire—a bounty that lacks nothing, and is never saturated. We will find the image of the flame again in another of Bernard's passages, according to this same paradox, it represents eternity, not as a static state, but as a stability in movement[15] (*Sermons for Sundays in November*, Sermon IV).

> Will the seraphs have to continue to fly in order to provide for each other's needs, free them from the perils which threaten them, help those who worry, comfort those who find themselves suffering? No, in the kingdom of eternal happiness, need, danger, worry, and suffering are barred. Why these wings? Because, in reality, this way of keeping firmly upright pleases me: I absolutely want to stay this way and I don't know how to envisage anything that could deprive me of this stability.
>
> However, I know, O blessed Isaiah, being a prophet (see Jn 4:19), you have the Holy Spirit of the One who, through the generosity of his bounty, surpasses not only that which man could merit, but all that he could wish for.
>
> May this desired stability be saved for me; but if these wings could add something to this happiness, I will not refuse them. Yet, I believe that immutability is promised to us through the fact that we stand upright, and that liveliness is promised to us through the fact that seraphs fly. In this way, we are kept to imagine a stability that is deprived of sensation and similar to that of a stone.
>
> "Seraphs were in attendance above him; each had six wings: with two they covered their faces, and with two they covered their feet, and with two they flew" (Isa 6:2). This phrase seems to show me what had been said about the firm stability that explains itself more clearly by the flight. In fact, where do the seraphs fly, if

not towards the One for whom they burn with love? Look at a flame: it is as if it flies by staying in the same place. Don't be surprised that the seraphs can fly without displacing themselves and remain still by flying.

The image of the flame is marvelously suggestive to evoke the coincidence of a stability and a dynamism. The fire symbolizes fervor, constant newness, the pull towards heaven that is in basic stability.

Bernard then questions himself about the meaning of the two wings which the seraphs use to fly. The reply that he proposes brings us, with happiness, to a theme that we have already seen in many of the previous chapters: the unity to be achieved between a more objective dimension, in us, of understanding, judgment brought by reason, or, like he said here, of "knowledge," and the more subjective dimension in us of the affectivity of desire, which, here, he calls "pietas" (the echo of fervor which faith awakens in the heart) or "love."

The wing of knowledge effectively lifts; but it alone is not enough. We will quickly collapse if we strive to fly with only one wing; and the higher we have risen, the more serious the fall will be. The pagan philosophers tried it, they who, even though "they knew God, did not honor him as God; they became futile in their thinking, and their senseless minds were darkened" (Rom 1:21). Given up to a debased mind (Rom 1:28), they ventured all the way to the most shameful passions, to the point of fully justifying this sentence: "Anyone, then, who knows the right thing to do and fails to do it, commits sin" (Jas 4:17).

In the same way, a zeal that is not enlightened (see

Rom 10:2), falls harder if it is precipitated with more impetuousness: it will only take off to fall again.

That reminds us of what we have seen with respect to the assimilation of God's Word: the link between meditation and prayer, through which the Word descends from the understanding into the heart and becomes our own. The simultaneous movement of the two wings, then, symbolizes this conversion of understanding by becoming faith, and of the affectivity becoming fervor and willingness. We thus evade two symmetrical dangers: this form of pride which is intellectualism, by serving as a pretext for faith that brings no fruit of life; and this temptation for religious sentimentalism which takes the place of faith.

To the contrary, when love accompanies understanding, and humble affection accompanies knowledge, we then fly in complete safety, we fly endlessly because we fly towards eternity.

REFLECTION QUESTIONS

Do I ever tire of seeking God? Can I conceive of terms such as infinite, immeasurable, and eternity? If God is infinite and I desire to know him completely, how could I ever tire of God? Do I recognize that while there will be a stability in heaven there will never be a lack of desire from myself towards God?

DAY THIRTEEN

Fraternal Love

FOCUS POINT

Perhaps the finest way to show our love for our God is to serve him a very concrete manner: by serving his creation, our fellow brothers and sisters. Jesus showed us the way to love, in service and compassion, and we are given the grace to love beyond our selfish desires, and put the needs of our brothers and sisters ahead of our own. This is love: extending our selves for the benefit of the other. In turn, we benefit as well.

We walk in procession, two by two, candles in our hands, (...) furthermore, in this procession, the first are the last. (...)
    Rightfully so, we advance two by two: as the saints of the gospels attested, this is the way that the Savior sent his disciples on missions (Mk 6:7), in order to bring to the forefront

fraternal love and communal life. The one who advances alone in the procession would be disruptive; he doesn't only bother himself, he annoys all of the others. Such is the way of those who marginalize themselves, "it is these worldly people, devoid of the Spirit, who are causing divisions" (Jude 19). They manifest no desire to "make every effort to maintain the unity of the Spirit in the bond of peace" (Eph 4:3)[16] (Sermon for the Purification of Mary, Sermon II).

W ith these words, Saint Bernard describes the celebration surrounding the feast of February 2, when the little Jesus was brought to the temple to be presented to the Lord. Formerly, the Church held a procession on that day (one that is still held in monasteries today). In his sermon for this feast day, Saint Bernard shows us the symbolism of this procession: the need for the sons and daughters of Christ to walk in the unity of the spirit and the bond of peace.

With reason, we hold onto our freedom, but perhaps without always adequately situating it. Does walking along with my brothers and sisters, in community life, jeopardize my freedom? Does renouncing to do what pleases me, which would marginalize me, make me lose something essential? Would it not also be, in the name of my freedom, as seen in more depth like a dimension of love, that I could decide to proceed at a communal rhythm and keep the unity of the spirit with others, instead of acting like an animal who only wants to do what he wants to do?

In other respects, along with what has been said about communal life and fraternal charity, good works and

holy fervor, this very great virtue of humility is sworn
to be necessary in the highest degree so that we know
to love one another in mutual affection (Rom 12:10),
and so that each one considers himself beneath the others, not just the elders, but the younger ones as well.
That is assurance for the perfection of humility and
the bounty of righteousness.[17]

Giving priority to everyone, even the younger ones, in such
a hierarchical society as ours, is asking a great deal—even more
than with Saint Benedict's Rule, which only demands honor
and respect for the elders. And what is remarkable is that Bernard calls this perfect humility, where I voluntarily pass after
everyone else, "the bounty of righteousness." Why? Because
Jesus, when he stepped forward to be baptized by John, who
felt that he was unworthy, replied to him that they would be
doing it "to fulfill all righteousness" (Mt 3:15)—the bounty of
righteousness. If righteousness consists of rendering what is
his due to each person (it is a classic and possible definition),
full and total righteousness will then be given to each person,
even if he doesn't have the right to it: like Jesus, with the same
interior freedom, the same lucidity, the same lavishness.

Does this break me down or devalue me? No, it is to want
what is best for others and, as much as possible, to promote
God's desire rather than my own, and to ensure to align my
desire to his. Is this not a form of conversion of desire?

Bernard spoke of this, in the following terms, one day when
he exhorted:

To maintain unity so well that, inserted in a community, you pass the will of others before your own. Not
only do you live amongst your brothers without com-

plaint, but with gratitude, supporting them and praying for them in such a way that we can also say of you
that: "This is a man who loves the family of Israel and
prays much for the people and the holy city of Jerusalem" (2 Macc 15:14).[18]

And if we want to stick very closely to this interior conversa-
tion, which, alone, permits a unity with our neighbor, we can
see that it is composed of two ideas, two spiritual actions: one
of going outside of yourself and uniting with the other person;
the other, one which we think about less, but which is equally
important, of trust and opening ourselves in order to allow
others to unite with and love us.

The unity that we put into action with our neighbor has
two methods of realization:

We have spoken about this unity which each person
realizes within themselves. Let us now approach the
one which we put into action with our neighbor. It also
has two methods of realization: the neighborly love by
which we reach out to other people, and the welcome
which, in return, we keep for the burst of love from
other people. There are also two obstacles: egocentrism
and suspicion. Egocentrism prohibits us from reaching
the heart of another person, and suspicion prevents us
from believing in the other person's love. The conse-
quences are: centered on ourselves, we do not love our
neighbor; suspicious, we do not think we are loved,
and, at the same time, the unity, which we must have
with another person, is rendered impossible. There is a
double charity that gives relief for this double illness:
the one in which a person does not insist on his own

way (1 Cor 13:5), and the one which believes all things (1 Cor 13:7).

May the egocentric person put forth a charity that does not insist on its own way and may he love his neighbor. May the suspicious person acquire a charity that believes all things without doubt, and believes in the love that others have for him.[19]

This is what I must ask for in my prayers: on the one hand, the freedom to not consider other people as instruments of my desire; and, on the positive side, to have a spirit, heart, understanding, and imagination which is awakened in order to seek his desire. On the other hand, I must pray for the freedom to not always be on the defensive, barricaded in distrust, as if all requests to me, all good deeds done for me, and all good will forces me into a situation of unacceptable dependance.

May God give us his generosity: it certainly reveals itself in the endless source of initiatives of his love; just as much as it is in his expectation of our prayer, our praise, and our fervent love.

It is true: actually, we so often try to justify or even excuse God for seeming to count on our praise and thanksgiving. He has no need for our songs of praise; it is only for our good that he asks them of us. Truly. Is a love which, deliberately, waits for nothing in return, authentic love? To pass, with regret, to reciprocity, but to love all the same: yes, that is a bonus of love. But to give without wanting anything is return, to serve by refusing to be served, that is to not know either how to give or to serve. And if bad things do happen to us, we do not project them onto God as a virtue: let us ask him to deliver us from them.

REFLECTION QUESTIONS

In what ways do I serve my brothers and sisters at present? At what times in my life do I find it the most difficult to see beyond my self and place the needs of a stranger before my own? In what new ways might I reach out and help my brothers and sisters in need? Are there programs in my parish and community that might give me the opportunity to reach outside my self and serve others so that I might praise and glorify God?

Preparing Oneself for Death

FOCUS POINT

Before the coming of Jesus Christ, and his passion and death, death was the end. As punishment for Adam's sin, death allowed no chance of union with God following this life. But Jesus conquered death, made it holy, reunited man with God by his sacrifice on the cross. Before, death was only sadness. Now, death is sadness and joy. It is still sadness, as we leave this earth and those we love. But there is joy now. There is rebirth, union with God in heaven for all eternity.

"Which of you desires life, and covets many days to enjoy good?" (Ps 34:12). In fact, the life we lead here on earth is

rather a death; no, it is not simply a life, but a mortal life. We say that a certain man is dying, when evidently he approaches death. Yet, what else do we do, when we begin to live, if we aren't approaching death and making ourselves die? Besides, no matter what, the days of this life appear short and evil (see Eph 5:16), attests the holy patriarch. We only truly live that when life is vivid and long; and the days are only good when they are limitless in length[20] (Sermon on the Psalm "Who Lives," Sermon XVII).

To Christians, today is a gift from God: it would be a sin to depreciate it. In as much as without it, without the joy it brings, we would have no way of thinking about eternal life and of rejoicing in it. Saint Bernard knew this and said so on occasion. But, in the light of a forceful desire which is directed at the promises of a full life close to God, we can also take a severe and critical look at our present life. This is exactly the recommendation that Bernard makes in his *Sermon on the Psalm "Who Lives."*

The advantage of such an outlook, maybe its only one, is to make relative the opposition which is so absolute and dramatic that we spontaneously see ourselves between life and death. If our life on earth, as seen with a certain bias, is a form of death, death itself, by that same reasoning, can be envisaged as something other than an end or a fall into nothingness. Present life then ceases to feel like a bunch of passing days, for our unhappiness: that are lost and fall into the past. We are invited to consider it as a route which makes sense only at its end, we are called to live as a function of that end and to prepare for it.

Here is the exhortation that drew Bernard's attention, in celebration of the martyrdom of Saints Peter and Paul:

> Let us strive, brothers, to live as the righteous lived, but let us long even more to die as they died (Num 23:10). Wisdom reveals the final end of the righteous (Wis 2:16), judging us there where she finds us.
>
> It is absolutely necessary that the end of our present life be consistent with the beginning of our future life; no difference is tolerated. As anyone who wants to sew or join two belts together knows, if I may put it this way, they prepare the ends which are to be joined to each other uniformly so they don't come apart, and take little care for the other parts. In the same way, I say to you, how spiritual a way of life would there be if our ultimate end were carnal, inwardly inconsistent with that spiritual life to come, for flesh and blood will not inherit the kingdom of God? (1 Cor 15:50).[21]

Are we not shocked to see in this text that our preparation for the end of our life, our death, is, in reality, a preparation to enter into the true life to come? We are not preparing to die, but to be arisen from the dead!

What a healthy way to explain this to us: careful, be vigilant, always keep your sights on the day and the hour so you don't miss the passage! But of what does this vigilance consist? Live the present in the light of this future—as much as possible—and in agreement with him. In this way, anticipate it vigorously. In this same measure, earthly death—let us realize that—loses its fearsome and dramatic aspect, so that it is only a passage.

"Son," says the wise man, "remember your final end, and you will not sin" (Sir 7:36). Because this recollection makes you extremely devout, let fear drive out sin (Sir 1:27), and do not be negligent.22

If one prepares for their final end, does it mean that they have to live in obsession, fear, or agitation? Absolutely not. Vigilance, taking care to do this properly, and living well are humble ways of putting oneself into a state of dependence and trusting God's mercy. For Bernard, the fear of God ceases to be a fear of God when it becomes internal fear and distrust of our impudent boasting:

There is no other way for us to prepare for the final end except to consciously reflect upon all the dangers which seem to threaten us; then put all of our effort into learning to feel more distrust concerning our own merits, and to commit ourselves to God's protection alone—with our heart's loving affection and our mind's purposeful intention—to the one whose good endowment and perfect gift (Jas 1:17) is a happy and precious death (Ps 116:15).23

However, physical death will not become soothing. Bernard, who "detests" it, calls it the "bloodthirsty beast" and "the most bitter of bitternesses." But it will not have the last word, it should have to return even the body that it takes from us. In fact, it no longer had the last word, since Christ vanquished it through his love, even if he doesn't stop it from striking again. It becomes precious when it claims a holy person, someone who lived the gospel, because for that person, it becomes *the door to life, the entrance to perfect tranquility. It is then justified to congratulate those who have passed through fire and water* (the trials on earth) *and who have been taken into the place of refreshment.*

What we have just evoked are Bernard's reactions when faced with the deaths of a very good friend, Saint Malachy, an Irish bishop, and that of his former prior, Dom Humbert.[24] From these reactions, we can discern a sort of psychological and spiritual itinerary, which, for him as well, constitutes a means of preparation for death: one must pass (never once and for all, but always anew) from a dramatic feeling to a spiritual conception of death. They are both realistic and important not to minimalize, nor maximalize neither, but to establish a dialogue within ourselves between them—a dialogue between our feelings and our faith where faith patiently evangelizes our feelings.

Is living on earth as a function of the promised, true life (which Bernard invited us to do), not fleeing from the present, distrusting it and finally not drawing something from it? That is not Bernard's idea. For him, this real attention to God's future is just the opposite, a manner to take control of the time and in this very control *to allow a certain image of eternity to be remodeled within us.*

The idea is an admirable one. Eternity doesn't appear to be the opposite of time, but like a reconciliation in it of the past, present, and future. From now on, we can then have a foreshadowing of this blessed reconciliation: when faith becomes wisdom within us, in order to dispose of the present, the critical intelligence to draw lessons from our past, and the foresight to prepare for our future.

The past teaches us about all of the dangers that threaten us (also—but Bernard doesn't mention much about it—about the infinite resource of God's patience). The present calls us to distrust our personal merits and put our trust in God's care. Finally, the conscience of the future will become, on our part, a humble burst of the spirit and the putting into action of a humble determination towards God, whose excellent gift, the perfect gift (Jas 1:17), is a happy and precious death (Ps 116:15).[25]

REFLECTION QUESTIONS

How do I view death? Do I have mixed feelings? Sadness and joy? Fear and anticipation? When someone close to me dies, do I feel sad for myself and for their loved ones, yet happy for them, now that they have been reborn into life everlasting? Am I prepared for the suffering and death I must encounter before I can be reborn? How can I prepare myself for this re-birth?

Humility and Greatness in Mary

FOCUS POINT

Mary is the ultimate example of humility among all the creatures of God. There was an open space in Mary and in that space was humility. The presence of this humility made no room for pride or selfishness. There was only room for God. That is the beauty of humility: it displaces such evils as pride and selfishness while making room for God. God found the perfect woman to serve as his mother: Mary, the model of humility.

[Elizabeth,] you affirm that, at the sound of my voice, your son [John the Baptist] quivered in rejoicing, but, as far as I [Mary] am concerned, it is "my spirit" which "rejoiced in God

*my Savior" (Lk 1:47). And your Son himself, since he is also
the friend of the Bride, rejoices greatly at the Bridegroom's
voice (Jn 3:29).*

*You called the one who believed blessed, but this faith and
happiness are due to the benevolent look which, from above,
was placed upon me. As a result, if all generations must say
that I am blessed, it is mainly because God has looked with
favor on the lowliness of his servant (Lk 1:48)*[26] *(Sermon for
the Sunday in the Octave of the Assumption).*

O n many occasions, we should have recognized that, in
Christ, and in God's eyes, humility and greatness are
less opposed to each other than united. For Saint Bernard, that
is essentially what characterized the Blessed Virgin's holiness.
All of her being, all her life, desired to be totally dedicated, in
total humility and self-abandon, to this grandeur, to this exceptional mystery of being the mother of the Lord, the mother
of God, the Word, in his Incarnation.

In the opening passage from Saint Bernard's *Sermon for
the Sunday in the Octave of the Assumption,* he tells how Mary
responded to her cousin Elizabeth when she, at the rejoicing of
the infant in her womb, recognized Mary for her divine mater-
nity, and proclaimed her as blessed.

In this humility is where Bernard's gaze of admiration for
Mary was found. He invites us to share this observation with
him:

In the meantime, brothers, must we think that Elizabeth, who is holy, made a mistake when the Holy Spirit
inspired her words? Assuredly not! Blessed are those

on whom God has looked with favor (Lk 1:48), but also blessed are those who believed (Lk 1:45). For here is the fruit of God's gaze upon her. Through an inexplicable knowledge of the Holy Spirit, such a greatness of soul came to add itself to such humility in order to reach the most secret place in the heart of the Virgin (...).

Thus, a humility as profound as this removes nothing from this greatness, which, as vast as it is, does nothing to diminish this humility. For as humble as Mary was in the idea she had of herself, she was also very great in the trust she had in God's promise. Also, considering herself as a modest servant (Lk 1:38), she never doubted having been chosen in the light of this incomprehensible mystery, this admirable exchange, this fathomless sacrament and to soon becoming—she knew it through faith—the true mother of God-made-man.

It is just to admire someone on the condition that we are not seized but put into action by this admiring gaze. We will see this unity, that the Holy Spirit wanted to fulfill in Mary, in her perfection and also in us, between humility and greatness of the soul. Humility takes nothing away from the boldness of faith, to the contrary, it multiplies it.

The incomparable gift of God's grace which operates in the hearts of the chosen ones is so great: humility does not deprive them of courage, and the greatness of the soul does not render them arrogant. To the contrary, the two realities mutually support each other so well that the greatness, without restricting itself to not engender pride, gives humility its maximum depth. As a result, we manifest much more fear and gratitude towards the Donor of all goods, without humility providing the least pretext of a lack of courage in return: the more we get into the habit of putting no trust in ourselves for the least of things, the more we will place our trust in the strength of God, even for the greater things.

For us, Mary will then be a sign, an example, a model, a point of reference for authentic holiness, because she brings it out into the open and she discretely invites us to it by giving us the taste and desire for it.

By reason of this grace from God, the miracle of the Holy Spirit, and by so admirably combining humility and greatness, for Bernard, Mary is a mediator. This is certainly not besides, or in addition to, Christ's mediation, but it is like a participation in this unique mediation, so much so that the Virgin wanted herself totally from Christ and for him. To turn ourselves towards her, to count upon the support and help of her prayers, by calling upon her holiness, is essentially turning ourselves towards her Son—or more exactly, towards the most divine in the human being that the Son and the Holy Spirit could realize. The mediation of Mary, in other words, is her love for her Son and his love for her. This is how Bernard expresses it in a prayer:

And now, Mother of mercy,
in the name of the burst of love from your
purest of spirits,
the moon (in which Bernard saw the symbol
of the Church),
the moon prostrates itself at your feet;

with fervent supplications, it calls to you,
for you have been made
a mediator in its favor
beside the sun of righteousness (Mal 4:2);
its desire is in your light,
to see the light (Ps 36:9),
and through your intervention,
to obtain the grace of the Sun.
For he loved you more than
any other creature,
and he beautified you,
clothing you with a robe of glory (Sir 6:31)
and placing on your head a beautiful crown
(see Ezek 16:12).
You are filled with grace (see Lk 1:28),
filled with heaven's dew,
leaning on the Beloved (Song 8:5),
overflowing with delights.
O Lady, feed your poor people today!
May the dogs eat the crumbs (see Mt 15:27)!
From your overflowing pitcher, give drink
not only to Abraham's servant,
but also to his camels (see Gen 24:19),
for you truly are the young girl chosen
and appointed in advance (see Gen 24:14)
to heaven,
he who is, above all,
God, blessed for all time. Amen.

REFLECTION QUESTIONS

In what ways can Mary teach me about humility? Do I seek to clear a space with humility so that I will be open to God's will? Can I, like Mary, set aside my will—what I see fit as necessary—so that the plan of God may take its rightful place? Do I pray for the intercession of Mary so that God's will might be done in my life? What areas of my life infringe on God's will taking priority in my life?

Notes

Note: All texts cited are extracts from Sermons written by Saint Bernard of Clairvaux, unless otherwise stated.

DAY ONE:
1. All texts cited in this chapter are from *Sermons For Christmas*, Sermon I, 1–4.

DAY TWO:
2. All texts cited in this chapter are from *Bernard of Clairvaux, Sermons for the Summer Season*, B.M. Kienzle (trans.), Cistercian Publications: Kalamazoo, MI, 1991, pp. 37–39; *Sermons for the Ascension*, Sermon III, 2–4.

DAY THREE:
3. *Life and Works of St. Bernard*, S.J. Eales, John Hodges: London, 1896; *Sermons for Advent*, Sermon V, 1–3, pp. 279–280.

DAY FOUR:

4. All texts cited in this chapter are from *Sermons for Lent*, Sermon IV, 3–4.

DAY FIVE:

5. Ibid, Sermon V, 5–6.

DAY SIX:

6. Ibid, Sermon V, 6–7.

DAY SEVEN:

7. Ibid, Sermon V, 7.
8. *Sermons for the Annunciation of the Lord*, Sermon III, 9.
9. Op Cit, Sermon I, 4.

DAY EIGHT:

10. All texts cited in this chapter are from *Sermons for the Harvest*, Sermon III, 4.

DAY NINE:

11. Ibid, Sermon I, 1–2.

DAY TEN:

12. All texts cited in this chapter are extracts from *Sermon on the Psalm "Who Lives,"* Sermon XVII, 3–4.

DAY ELEVEN:

13. All texts cited in this chapter are from *Sermons For Sundays in November*, Sermon I, 1–2.

DAY TWELVE:

14. *Sermons About the Canticles*, Sermon 84, 1.

15. The remaining texts in this chapter are from *Sermons For Sundays in November*, Sermon IV, 1–2.

DAY THIRTEEN:

16. *Sermon For the Purification of Mary*, Sermon II, 1 and 2.

17. Ibid, 3.

18. *Sermon for the Christmas Vigil*, III, 6.

19. *Sermon for the Assumption of the Blessed Virgin Mary*, Sermon V, 13.

DAY FOURTEEN:

20. *Sermon on the Psalm "Who Lives,"* Sermon XVII, 1.

21. *Bernard of Clairvaux, Sermons for the Summer Season*, B.M. Kienzle (trans.), Cistercian Publications: Kalamazoo, MI, 1991, pp. 107, 108; *Sermon for the Solemn Feast of Apostles Peter and Paul*, Sermon II, 6.

22. Ibid, Sermon II, 7.

23. Ibid.

24. As reported in the *Sermon at the Time of the Passage of St. Malachy*, 4, 7; and in the *Sermon at the Time of the Death of Dom Humbert*, 3.

25. Op Cit, Sermon II, 7.

DAY FIFTEEN:

26. All of the texts cited in this chapter are from *Sermon for the Sunday in the Octave of the Assumption*, 12–13, 15.